CAMBRIDGE LIBRARY COLLECTION

Books of enduring scholarly value

Religion

For centuries, scripture and theology were the focus of prodigious amounts of scholarship and publishing, dominated in the English-speaking world by the work of Protestant Christians. Enlightenment philosophy and science, anthropology, ethnology and the colonial experience all brought new perspectives, lively debates and heated controversies to the study of religion and its role in the world, many of which continue to this day. This series explores the editing and interpretation of religious texts, the history of religious ideas and institutions, and not least the encounter between religion and science.

Testimonies

In this two-volume work, J. Rendel Harris (1852–1941) fundamentally shaped Biblical scholarship in the twentieth century, arguing for the existence of a 'first known treatise on Christian theology', antedating the New Testament. A palaeographer, Harris examined recurring textual corruptions of Old Testament passages in early Christian writers and surmised an underlying collection, which he called the 'Testimony Book'. The book, Harris believed, collected Biblical testimonia – passages prophesying Christ – in order to prove the legitimacy of the new Christian faith. These arguments against Judaic theology marked, in Harris's opinion, the beginnings of the Christian written tradition. Volume 1 (1916) lays the groundwork for Harris's argument by examining the use of testimonia in early Christian writers like Cyprian and Gregory of Nyssa. 'The starting point of the modern study of the use of the Old Testament in the New', this is a work of enduring importance to religion scholars.

T0345434

Cambridge University Press has long been a pioneer in the reissuing of out-of-print titles from its own backlist, producing digital reprints of books that are still sought after by scholars and students but could not be reprinted economically using traditional technology. The Cambridge Library Collection extends this activity to a wider range of books which are still of importance to researchers and professionals, either for the source material they contain, or as landmarks in the history of their academic discipline.

Drawing from the world-renowned collections in the Cambridge University Library, and guided by the advice of experts in each subject area, Cambridge University Press is using state-of-the-art scanning machines in its own Printing House to capture the content of each book selected for inclusion. The files are processed to give a consistently clear, crisp image, and the books finished to the high quality standard for which the Press is recognised around the world. The latest print-on-demand technology ensures that the books will remain available indefinitely, and that orders for single or multiple copies can quickly be supplied.

The Cambridge Library Collection brings back to life books of enduring scholarly value (including out-of-copyright works originally issued by other publishers) across a wide range of disciplines in the humanities and social sciences and in science and technology.

Testimonies

VOLUME 1

J. RENDEL HARRIS
ASSISTED BY VACHER BURCH

CAMBRIDGE UNIVERSITY PRESS

Cambridge, New York, Melbourne, Madrid, Cape Town,
Singapore, São Paolo, Delhi, Tokyo, Mexico City

Published in the United States of America by Cambridge University Press, New York

www.cambridge.org
Information on this title: www.cambridge.org/9781108039697

© in this compilation Cambridge University Press 2012

This edition first published 1916
This digitally printed version 2012

ISBN 978-1-108-03969-7 Paperback

TESTIMONIES

CAMBRIDGE UNIVERSITY PRESS
C. F. CLAY, Manager
London: FETTER LANE, E.C.
Edinburgh: 100 PRINCES STREET

New York: G. P. PUTNAM'S SONS
Bombay, Calcutta and Madras: MACMILLAN AND Co., Ltd.
Toronto: J. M. DENT AND SONS, Ltd.
Tokyo: THE MARUZEN-KABUSHIKI-KAISHA

TESTIMONIES

by

RENDEL HARRIS

with the assistance of

VACHER BURCH

PART I

Cambridge :
at the University Press
1916

INTRODUCTION

THE following pages are in part accumulated from the Journals in which I have been in the habit of drawing attention to the question of Testimonies against the Jews in the Early Church. It is not, however, the case that nothing fresh is to be found in this little volume. There is new matter of the highest importance to the theologian and to the student of Christian literature. It contains a proof (hitherto unsuspected) of the existence of an Apostolic work, which passed into obscurity: and directions are pointed out for the actual recovery of its contents. The work in question is the first known treatise on Christian theology. I need not emphasize further the importance of the matter. In the production and editing of these pages I have had the co-operation of Mr Vacher Burch, who has written two of the chapters (marked with his initials), and has carefully revised the volume, and the indexes which have been prepared by my secretary, Miss Irene Speller.

I am indebted to Messrs Hodder & Stoughton for permission to reproduce freely from the pages of the *Expositor*.

R. H.

September, 1916.

CONTENTS

CHAPTER I

THE USE OF TESTIMONIES IN THE EARLY CHRISTIAN CHURCH

INTRODUCTION.

Existence of Books of Testimonies Suspected.

The existence in the early Church of collections of Testimonies, extracted from the Old Testament for use against the Jews, has for a long time been a matter of suspicion. It was in the highest degree probable that such collections should arise, and their value for controversial purposes was so obvious that they would readily pass into the form of written books, and be subject to the correction, amplification, or excision of editors in such a way as to constitute in themselves a cycle of Patristic literature, the main lines of whose development can easily be traced and the variations thereof from one period of Church life to another can often be detected. They arose out of the exigency of controversy, and therefore covered the wide ground of canonical Jewish literature; but they were, at the same time, subject to the exigency of the controversialist, who, travelling from place to place, could not carry a whole library with him. It was, therefore, *a priori*, probable that they would be little books of wide range. The parallel which suggests itself to one's mind is that of the little handbook known as the Soldier's Pocket Bible, which was carried by the Ironsides of Cromwell, and was composed of a series of Biblical extracts, chiefly from the Old Testament, defining the duty of the Puritan soldier in the various circumstances in which he found himself, and arranged under the headings of questions appropriate to the situation.

As we have said, these collections have been suspected to exist by a number of students of early Patristic literature, though, as we hope to show, they have not, all of them, adequately realized the antiquity of the first forms in which Testimonies were circulated. It will be proper to draw attention to the way in which these suspicions have been expressed.

For example, the late Dr Hatch, in his *Essays on Biblical Greek*, wrote as follows[1]:

It may naturally be supposed that a race which laid stress on moral progress, whose religious services had variable elements of both prayer and praise, and which was carrying on an *active propaganda*, would have, among other books, *manuals* of morals, of devotion and of *controversy*. It may also be supposed, if we take into consideration the contemporary habit of making collections of *excerpta*, and the special authority which the Jews attached to their sacred books, that some of these manuals would consist of extracts from the Old Testament. The existence of composite quotations in the New Testament and in some of the early Fathers suggests the hypothesis that we have in them relics of such manuals.

Manuals of controversy, such as Dr Hatch imagines to be the apparatus of a Jewish missionary in early times, might perhaps be described as *Testimonia pro Judaeis*, and, if such existed, there is nothing to forbid their having been produced by the Hellenists of the prae-Christian period, as well as by those of a later date. What we are concerned with, however, is not *Testimonies on behalf of the Jews*, whose force would not be very great except with those who were already well on the way to conviction of the truth of Judaism; but *Testimonies against Jews*, of the nature of a series of *argumenta ad hominem*, where the man was identified with his own religion and then refuted from it. And it is only necessary to say here of the very illuminating sentence quoted from Dr Hatch, that if such collections of Testimonies on behalf of the Jews existed in early times, before the diffusion of Christianity, then there must have been, *a fortiori*, similar collections produced in later times, when the Christian religion was being actively pushed by the Church in the Synagogue. It is, of course, possible also that those phenomena on which Hatch's observations turned, such as the early existence of composite quotations from the Septuagint, may belong to the class of Testimonies *against* the Jews, and not to Testimonies *on behalf of* them. In which case the error in not recognizing their character would be due to the want of a right sense of the antiquity of this form of Christian propaganda.

---

[1] Hatch, *loc. cit.* p. 203.

Harnack alludes to Hatch's work in an appreciative manner in his *History of Dogma*[1] and says:

Hatch has taken up again the hypothesis of earlier scholars, that there were very probably in the first and second centuries systematized extracts from the Old Testament. The hypothesis is not yet quite established (see Wrede, *Untersuchungen zum 1 Clemensbrief*, p. 65), but yet it is hardly to be rejected. The Jewish catechetical and missionary instruction in the Diaspora needed such collections, and their existence seems to be proved by the Christian Apologies and the Sibylline books.

In his work on the *Character and Authorship of the Fourth Gospel*, Dr Drummond has expressed the same suspicion, though with a modest apology for wandering into the region of conjecture. He is pointing out[2] the difficulties into which the successive translators of the Old Testament into Greek were driven by the necessarily controversial use which was to be made of their translations.

"It may have become," says he, "a matter of common knowledge among those who cared for the Scriptures, that certain passages required emendation. The Christians would naturally turn their attention chiefly to Messianic quotations; and *it is conceivable that there may have grown up, whether in writing or not, an anthology of passages useful in controversy,* which differed more or less from the current Greek translation. This is, of course, only conjecture; but I think it affords a possible explanation of the phenomena of the Johannine quotations."

This also is an illuminating statement; it recognizes that collections of Messianic passages may have antedated the Fourth Gospel, and that they may have been written collections, made by Christians. If the hypothesis is a correct one, then we are very near indeed to the suggestion that *Testimonies against the Jews* are amongst the earliest deposits of the Christian literature.

Early Collections of Testimonies against the Jews are still extant.

When we begin to explore into the region of Christian literature for evidences as to the formal use of Old Testament prophecies in controversies with the Jews, we find the confirmation required, not only in the case of composite quotations, such as those to which Dr Hatch refers, or Messianic prophecies such as Dr Drum-

---

[1] Vol. I. p. 175 (Eng. Tr.).   [2] Drummond, *loc. cit.* p. 365.

mond speaks of, but in the survival of a number of early Christian books, which are hardly more than strings of Anti-Jewish texts with editorial connexions and arrangements.   We are not limited to a search in the pages of early Christian polemists, such as Justin or Irenaeus, though, as we shall show presently, there is abundance of fragmentary matter in their writings which can best be explained by the use of a book of Testimonies, and, indeed, in such a case as that of Justin, whose largest and most important work is a debate, real or imaginary, with a Jewish Rabbi, it would be strange indeed if Justin did not use the method of Testimonies, while the rest of the Church used them freely.   It is not, however, a question of isolating quotations and reconstructing the books from which they were taken.   There are a number of such books actually extant, which, when read side by side, show, from their common matter and method, and from their curious and minute agreements, that they constitute the very cycle of literature which we have been speaking of under the name of *Testimonies*; that is, they are definite books of polemic, closely connected one with the others, and bearing marks of derivation from a common original.

In the case of a writer who uses Testimonies freely we may find ourselves in a difficulty as to whether he should be classed with Patristic writers, like Justin, who use Testimonies, but only in the course of an argument, or whether he should be grouped with Cyprian and others, to whom the Testimonies are the argument itself and not mere incidents in the course of it.   But this is only a question of degree.   All writers who can be convicted of the use of a *Testimony Book* will be in evidence for the reconstruction of that book, in one or other of the phases of its evolution.

We have already alluded to the case of Cyprian, and from the distinction drawn above, if it could be maintained, between those who quote and those who merely edit or transcribe such books, we should be led to say that there are, from that point of view, two Cyprians; one who uses a book of Testimonies like Justin, for incidental polemic, and the other who makes, on his own account, an edition of the book with expansions and changes from his own editorial hand.   The first may conveniently be neglected, at all events for the present.   The second is one of our prime authorities.

Cyprian's Testimonies contain an earlier collection of Testimonies against the Jews.

A reference to the complete works of Cyprian will show a work in three books, addressed to a certain Quirinus, and headed with the title *Testimonia*. Of these the third book is concerned with Christian ethics and is clearly a later addition to the other two. But the first two books have a common preface in which Cyprian explains to Quirinus that he has put together two little tracts; one to show that the Jews, according to prophecy, have lost the Divine favour and that the Christians have stepped into their place; and the other to show that Christ was, and is, what the Scripture foretold Him to be. And the direct attack upon the Jews in the first book, followed by the appeal to them which is involved in the prophecies (from the Old Testament) of the second book, is sufficient to permit us to re-write the title of Cyprian's book from the simple form *Testimonia* into the form *Testimonia adversus Judaeos*; or, at all events, to regard the longer title as latent in the shorter.

We shall have to refer constantly to these two books in the course of our investigation, both to the actual quotations made, and to the heads under which they are grouped. No one will doubt that we have rightly described the books if he will read the capitulations, beginning with the statement that

The Jews have gravely offended God,

and concluding with the affirmation that

The Gentiles who believe are more than the Jews,

and that

The Jews can only obtain forgiveness by admission to the Christian Church.

There can be no doubt that in Cyprian's writings we have preserved a book of Testimonies against the Jews.

Tertullian against the Jews is a mass of Quotations, probably from an early Book of Testimonies.

A somewhat similar case will be the tract ascribed to Tertullian, which goes under the name of *Tertullianus adversus Judaeos*. We shall be able, quite easily, to show the book of Testimonies underlying this tract of Tertullian's; the matter is, however, somewhat complicated by critical questions which have arisen as to the unity of the authorship of the work. It is, however, generally conceded that the first eight chapters are from Tertullian's hand, and that the remainder is largely made up out of his other writings (possibly by the expansion of a later and less-skilled hand).

The book opens out for us a vista in another direction. We are told in the preface that it arose out of an unsatisfactory and inconclusive public debate between a Christian (Tertullian himself?) and a Jewish proselyte; and that it was an attempt to clear up the matters in dispute between them. Now there is a whole region of Christian literature, most of it unhappily lost, which was made up of dialogues between real or imaginary Christian and Jewish debaters; and we may take it for granted that many of the proof-texts which we find in the book of Testimonies will appear also in such dialogues as those of Jason and Papiscus, Simon and Theophilus, Aquila and Timothy; and that these works and similar ones, where extant, will be in evidence for the restoration which we are trying to make. In reality, however, they constitute a cycle of their own, and should be treated separately.

The case of Tertullian against the Jews does not properly belong with these, as it is not cast in the form of a dialogue, and follows closely the lines of the collectors of *Testimonia*. And it will be sufficient here to state that it will be found very useful in determining the contents and defining the antiquity of the early *Testimonia*.

Gregory of Nyssa is credited with a Book of Testimonies against the Jews.

A third and most important collection is one which passes under the name of Gregory of Nyssa, and which was published by Zacagni in his *Collectanea Sacra*. Whether the ascription of authorship is rightly made may be a difficult matter to decide. For, as soon as we have agreed that the excerpts which make up the collection are conventional and traditional, we have very little to test the authorship by; in so far as they are excerpts, we have Gregory of Nyssa as an editor and not as an author. In that case only the headings will tell us of the authorship; we have not, as in Cyprian's case, the guidance or confirmation which comes from the fact of the collection being in Old Latin. But, on the other hand, if the matter be traditional and the parallels can be found all over the first three centuries, there is no reason why the ascription to Gregory of Nyssa should be false. What possible motive can be assigned for such an ascription of authorship, except that the book was found amongst his writings? and if it was thus found, it is not impossible that it may have had his editorial care, just as did the Cyprianic collection. However, it does not really matter whose collection it is, and we can cite it as Gregory of Nyssa without any prejudice to the question of ultimate authorship. We shall find many features in the work which are certainly of high antiquity and can be paralleled from the Fathers of the first three centuries.

Bar Ṣalibi Against the Jews.

And last of all we come to the treatise of Bar Salibi *Against the Jews*, which, though late in date, contains many relics of the earlier controversies, and probably whole sections, slightly disguised by their transference into Syriac, of the lost book that we are in quest of. We have no need to apologize for Bar Salibi's late date, relatively to such writers as Tertullian, Cyprian or Nyssen. It is recognized that the writings of Bar Salibi contain a great deal of early matter. We have not only had to thank him for his share in the vindication of the Diatessaron of Tatian and of Ephrem's commentary upon it, but we have also had his evidence for the reality of the Gaius with whom Hippolytus disputed (though Lightfoot made Gaius into a shadow of Hippolytus himself) and for a number of valuable extracts from the lost book against Gaius; to say nothing of the suggestion which he supplied that the celebrated Canon of Muratori was a fragment from that very book. Bar Salibi must have had an excellent library of early Fathers at his disposal, and it is very likely that more will yet be found of lost Christian authors in his pages. This new tract, then, of Bar Ṣalibi can easily be proved to belong to the same cycle as the other books of which we have been speaking.

We will now show how the conjecture of the critics, and the evidence of the extant literature, as to the existence of early books of Testimonies, can be confirmed by the internal evidence of the books referred to, including, of course, Bar Salibi himself.

Evidence for Books of Testimonies.

Probably the best way to arrange the internal evidence which the extant books of Testimonies and the early Christian writers furnish for the construction of a lost original document or documents, would be to arrange the matter under some such scheme as the following:

(*a*) *Peculiar Texts.* We should carefully note the recurrence of those various readings which appear to be unique in such collections and such arguments as we have been alluding to.

(*b*) *Recurrent Sequences.* We should carefully study the sequence of the passages which are adduced in the same collections and arguments. We shall find that sequences recur, just as readings do.

(*c*) *Erroneous Authorship.* We shall also find that there is a recurrence of erroneous ascriptions of authorship, by which a wrong title is assigned to a passage taken from the Old Testament.

(*d*) *Editor's Prefaces, Comments and Questions.* We shall find a recurrence of introductory or explanatory clauses which betray the hand of an editor or collector, and of which not a few belong to the very first strata of the deposited testimonies.

(*e*) *Matter for the use of the Controversialist.* We shall find that these explanatory and introductory clauses are often of the nature of direct challenges such as would be made in a debate, or would be considered as applicable to the person or persons for whom the book is intended.

Now let us give some instances that will come under these various heads, without attempting to follow a strict logical order; and we shall readily illustrate the arguments that must have been involved in the conventional oral or written statements which the early Christians made to the Jews with whom they were contending; and it will soon become as clear as daylight that the major part of the Testimonies in question were not limited to oral circulation, but that they were extant in book form.

Suppose, for example, we were reading the following passage in Irenaeus[1] relating to certain prophecies about our Lord:

Qui autem dicunt, adventu ejus *quemadmodum cervus claudus saliet, et plana erit lingua mutorum et aperientur oculi caecorum, et aures surdorum audient,* et manus dissolutae, et genua debilia firmabuntur; et, *resurgent qui in monumento sunt mortui,* et ipse *infirmitates nostras accipiet et languores portabit*; eas quae ab eo curationes fiebant annuntiaverunt:

and if we were to place side by side with this the following passage from Justin's *First Apology*[2]:

῞Οτι δὲ καὶ θεραπεύσειν πάσας νόσους καὶ νεκροὺς ἀνεγερεῖν ὁ ἡμέτερος Χριστὸς προεφητεύθη, ἀκούσατε τῶν λελεγμένων. ῎Εστι δὲ ταῦτα. Τῇ παρουσίᾳ αὐτοῦ ἁλεῖται χωλὸς ὡς ἔλαφος καὶ τρανὴ ἔσται γλῶσσα μογιλάλων· τυφλοὶ ἀναβλέψουσι καὶ λεπροὶ καθαρισθήσονται καὶ νεκροὶ ἀναστήσονται καὶ περιπατήσουσιν·

we should at once see that both Justin and Irenaeus have added an introductory formula to the quotation which they make from Isaiah xxxv., and this introductory formula, "at his advent," ought to have been italicized in Irenaeus as a part of the quotation; in other words, it is not, in either case, an immediate quotation from Isaiah, but a quotation from a book containing Testimonies of Isaiah and others. For no one will for a moment assume that Irenaeus went to Justin's writings in search of the introductory formula. He found it attached to his prophecies, as Justin did. The words had been substituted for the introductory "then" in "then shall the lame man leap, etc.," as if a question had been asked and answered with regard to the time implied by the prophet. The answer itself is due to the previous sentence (Isa. xxxv. 4), "Your God will come...He will come and save you."

Moreover we have with the quotation a decided suggestion that the prophecies quoted were grouped under heads, and we can come near to the restoration of one such formula. For when Irenaeus introduces the matter, he does it by a statement that "those who say thus and thus...announced the cures which were done by him (sc. Christ)." And Justin says, "Now that he was to heal diseases and to raise the dead may be seen from the following prophecies." Looking back to Irenaeus' quotation we see that he also has the raising of the dead along with the cures, though he does not use the same proof-text; and on turning to

[1] Lib. ɪv. 55. 2; ed. Mass. 273.   [2] 1 *Ap.* 48.

another chapter of the *Apology* of Justin (c. 54), we find the complaint made that when the heathen "learnt that it was foretold that he should *heal diseases and raise the dead,* they dragged in Asklepius" to explain the facts. Here again we catch the refrain of the introductory formula, "That it was foretold of Christ that He should heal diseases, etc."

Last of all, we notice that the quotation of Irenaeus is a series of extracts or Testimonies. It is a composite quotation. He begins with Isaiah xxxv. 5, 6, goes on with Isaiah xxvi. 19, and concludes with Isaiah liii. 4; this is just what we should expect from a collection of Testimonies. And we conclude, therefore, that both Irenaeus and Justin had access to such a collection and probably it was a part of their Christian education to know such a book.

Now let us try a somewhat similar passage from Irenaeus of which we have the Greek preserved. In the third volume of the Oxyrhynchus papyri, Grenfell and Hunt gave a series of seven fragments from an unknown Christian writer, with the interesting statement that the fragments might be as old as the second century. These fragments were promptly identified by Dr Armitage Robinson as containing portions of the lost Greek text of Irenaeus, and with the aid of the extant Latin he restored very skilfully the order and completed the contents of the passages involved in the torn fragments of papyrus. Amongst his restorations one passage corresponding to the Latin of Irenaeus, Bk III. c. 9, ran as follows: a few letters in each line being the key to the passage:

. . . . . . οὗ καὶ τὸ ἄ-	i.e., of whose star
στρον Βαλαὰμ μὲν οὔ]τως ἐ-	Balaam prophesied
προφήτευσεν ᾿Ανατε]λ[εῖ ἄ	as follows: There
στρον ἐξ ᾿Ιακώβ . . .]	shall rise a star
	out of Jacob, etc.

To this restoration I took exception on two grounds: (1) that the Clermont and Vossian copies of Irenaeus read in the Latin, not Balaam, but *Isaiah*; (2) that the same mistake of crediting Isaiah with a passage from Numbers was made in the following passage of Justin (1 *Apol.* c. 32):

καὶ ῾Ησαίας δὲ, ἄλλος προφήτης, τὰ αὐτὰ δι' ἄλλων ῥήσεων προφητεύων οὕτως εἶπεν· ᾿Ανατελεῖ ἄστρον ἐξ ᾿Ιακώβ, καὶ ἄνθος ἀναβήσεται ἀπὸ τῆς ῥίζης ᾿Ιεσσαὶ κτέ.

From this passage we see how the error of placing the name of Isaiah on a prophecy of Balaam arose; for Justin shows us the passage of Isaiah following the one from Numbers, and the error lies in the covering of two passages with a single reference. It is clear, then, that Justin's mistake was made in a collection of Testimonies from the prophets, and that the same collection, or one that closely agreed with it, was in the hands of Irenaeus. We have thus confirmed our results in a previous case, and can proceed with confidence, assuming not only the existence, but also the extreme antiquity of the collections referred to.

We have now illustrated the recurrence of quotations in a given sequence and the displacement of the names of prophets quoted, to which we referred above as furnishing the internal tests for the use of Testimony books.

As the field of criticism, which is thus opened up, is very wide, and the suspicion arises in our minds that there is matter of the same kind in the New Testament itself, it will be worth our while to give a few illustrations more, by which we may confirm the external and internal evidence for the lost books and tracts of which we are speaking. There is a remarkable reading, apparently from the Greek Psalter, which has perplexed the souls of many critics who have set themselves to find either the authority for the reading or an explanation of its genesis. I refer to the famous passage in which the early Fathers speak of Christ under the terms, "The Lord reigned from the tree."

Of the antiquity of the text there can be no doubt; it is certainly earlier than Justin, and it would not require a very acute imagination to suggest that it was involved in the argument of St Peter with the Jewish rulers in Acts v. 30, 31, where we are told that—

> Ye slew Him and hanged Him on *a tree*;
> Him hath God exalted *a Prince* and a Saviour.

But whether it is involved in the text of Acts or not, it is well known that it is one of the passages which Justin accused the men of the Synagogue of having erased from the Biblical text; that is, it was an obvious *argumentum ad Judaeum*. We make the suggestion that the passage never occurred in any MS. of the LXX, but that Justin took it from a book of Testimonies. He introduces it as being from the 95th Psalm[1]; which suggests

---

[1] Justin, *Dial.* 73.

either a reference to the Psalter or to a book of extracts which
introduced a sentence somewhat in the following manner:

> David in the 95th Psalm: "Say among the heathen, the Lord reigned
> from the tree."

According to Justin the last three words had been removed
from the LXX by the Jews. Is this a mere guess on Justin's
part? Let us see if we can get any light on the matter.

The next writer who quotes the passage is, I think, Tertullian
Against the Jews (c. 10); we have already alluded to this tract
as containing many of the earliest Testimonies employed by the
Christians of the first two centuries. He introduces it, along
with many other references to the Cross and Passion, as follows:

> Age dum, si legisti penes Prophetam in psalmis, *Deus regnavit a ligno*:
> expecto quid intelligas, etc.

This is thoroughly in the manner of the controversialist, and
suggests the use of a conventional method. The debater asks
his opponent what he makes of this text. Can we find confirmation for the suggestion that we are dealing with formal matter
definitely arranged? I think we can.

The passage quoted from Justin is only one out of a number
of texts which he says the Jews have altered. Curiously they
all belong to the same category, viz., prophecies of the Cross and
Passion. The one which precedes this one that we are discussing
is the well-known statement that the Jews have removed (though
it is still to be found in some copies) a passage in which Jeremiah
said, "Come, let us put wood on His bread," the wood being
assumed to be the Cross. Now this is quoted in the Testimonies
of Gregory of Nyssa in the following form:

Ἰερεμίας. Ἐγὼ δὲ ὡς ἀρνίον ἄκακον ἀγόμενον τοῦ θύεσθαι, οὐκ ἔγνων.

καὶ πάλιν. Δεῦτε καὶ ἐμβαλῶμεν ξύλον εἰς τὸν ἄρτον αὐτοῦ καὶ ἐκτρίψωμεν
αὐτὸν ἀπὸ τῶν ζώντων καὶ τὸ ὄνομα αὐτοῦ οὐ μὴ μνησθῇ ἔτι.

If with this we compare the quotation of the same passage by
Bar Ṣalibi (p. 33), we have as follows:

> And Jeremiah: And I was like an innocent lamb that is led to the
> slaughter, and I did not know what was over me[1]. And come, let us corrupt (?)
> wood on his bread[2].

[1] A reference to p. 23, where the passage is quoted again, suggests that this
should read, "And I did not know: and against me [they devised devices] and
said, Come, let us corrupt his bread on the wood." That is, some words have
dropped on p. 33, and a slight transposition has been made on p. 23; the existence
of a common original for the two quotations is sufficiently evident.

[2] Both of the passages are in Cyprian, *Test.* II. 15, and the second of the two
passages is in Cyprian, *Test.* II. 20.

Here two separate collections of Testimonies make the very same sequence of supposed passages from Jeremiah, and it is clear that they reflect a primitive arrangement and ascription of the peculiar words. But this ascription is Justin's, and it seems to be probable that Justin was using his *Testimony Book*, and not his copy of the Septuagint, when he talked about "the wood and the bread." If this is likely for one of the passages which the Jews are said to have altered, then, since they all deal with the subject of the Cross, they probably were all taken from a book of prophecies which had been fulfilled, arranged under various heads. In that case, Justin's reference to the Jews as destroying or removing texts is gratuitous. And that it is so is clear in the case of "the wood and the bread" from the fact that all copies of the LXX have the disputed reading in Jeremiah xi. 19. If Justin had looked at any Greek copy of Jeremiah, he would have found it; but he looked instead at the *Testimony Book*, and assumed that it was absent from Jeremiah (unless in a few cases it had escaped correction).

The development of pertinent questions in connexion with prophetical quotations is a subject that covers a great deal of ground. It is clear that many of these questions belong to the very earliest form of the *Testimony Book*. For example, when we read in Irenaeus (lib. IV. c. xx. 2) as follows:

Jam autem et manifestaverat [sc. Moyses] ejus adventum, dicens: *Non deerit princeps in Juda, neque dux ex femoribus ejus, quoadusque veniat cui repositum est, et ipse est spes gentium ; alligans ad vitem pullum suum et ad helicem pullum asinae. Lavabit in vino stolam suam, et in sanguine uvae pallium suum ; laetifici oculi ejus a vino et candidi dentes ejus quam lac.* Inquirant enim hi qui omnia scrutari dicuntur, id tempus in quo defecit princeps et dux ex Juda:

we have one of the greatest of the Messianic proof-texts, accompanied by a question as to when the ruler failed from the line of Judah. Suppose now we turn to Justin's *First Apology* (c. 32); here we are told as follows:

Μωϋσῆς μὲν οὖν, πρῶτος τῶν προφητῶν γενόμενος, εἶπεν αὐτολεξεὶ οὕτως· Οὐκ ἐκλείψει ἄρχων ἐξ Ἰούδα οὐδὲ ἡγούμενος ἐκ τῶν μηρῶν αὐτοῦ, ἕως ἂν ἔλθῃ ᾧ ἀπόκειται· καὶ αὐτὸς ἔσται προσδοκία ἐθνῶν, δεσμεύων πρὸς ἄμπελον τὸν πῶλον αὐτοῦ, πλύνων ἐν αἵματι σταφυλῆς τὴν στολὴν αὐτοῦ. Ὑμέτερον οὖν ἐστιν ἀκριβῶς ἐξετάσαι καὶ μαθεῖν, μέχρι τίνος ἦν ἄρχων καὶ βασιλεὺς ἐν Ἰουδαίοις ἴδιος αὐτῶν.

Here we have substantially the same quotation, followed by a similar inquiry; the connexion between the two statements is further established by the curious coincidence that both writers refer the quotation to Moses, and not to Jacob[1]. We shall see later that Athanasius does the very same thing: καὶ Μωϋσῆς ἕως αὐτοῦ τὴν Ἰουδαίων ἵστασθαι βασιλείαν προφητεύει λέγων (*De Incarn.* c. 40, following the text of the Bodleian MS. Other MSS. corr. *Moses* to *Jacob*).

The coincidences are such that we are entitled to say that the early *Testimony Book* referred the prophecy of Jacob to Moses, and accompanied it by a pertinent query. And many similar conjunctions can be noted. Perhaps the most important of them, from a theological point of view, may be found in the treatment to which a certain verse from the 110th Psalm was subjected, and the questions that were asked in connexion with it. When one reads the history of the great Council of Nicaea for the first time, the feeling of impressiveness, which is provoked by the historical scene and by the greatness of its theme of debate, is tempered by astonishment at the inadequacy of many of the arguments which are brought forward, and with the utmost seriousness considered, with a view to the determination of the proper language in which to clothe the doctrine of the Sonship of Jesus Christ. With a subject for discourse such as for sacredness and high solemnity has never been equalled in the history of human thought, and with a congress of intellects involving at least two or three religious teachers whose capacity far outreaches the average human span, it is surprising that the issue of the great contest should turn so much on misinterpreted texts and overstrained similitudes. It almost seems as if the combatants were giants and children by turns, or as if they held briefs to reproduce not only the loftiest thoughts of the teachers of the Church in earlier ages, but also their weakest suggestions along with the chatter of the baths and of the bakers' shops. What are we to make of Athanasius when he uses, to determine the language of the Church's Symbol of Faith, a verse from the 110th Psalm, in which we read in the Greek version:

πρὸ ἑωσφόρου γεγέννηκά σε.
(Before the day-star I begat thee.)?

---

[1] So in Justin, 1 *Apol.* c. 54, the Messianic prophecy is again referred to Moses. But in *Dial.* 54 he explains that the passages are recorded by Moses, but prophesied by Jacob: ὑπὸ Μωϋσέως ἀνιστορημένον καὶ ὑπὸ τοῦ πατριάρχου Ἰακὼβ προπεφητευμένον.

It seems almost inconceivable that so much can have been made of a misinterpreted and mistranslated text. Yet no one seems to have questioned that the passage was germane to the discussion: the only question was as to the extent to which the Church was committed by its assumed oracle. No one questioned the accuracy of the Septuagint reading, nor its applicability to either the Homoousion or the Homoiousion doctrine.

When, however, we succeed, however imperfectly, in transferring ourselves into the fourth century so as to be able to look both up-stream and down-stream at the flowing doctrine of the Church, we can see that the very fact of the influence of the passage quoted proves that it was not quoted for the first time at the Council of Nicaea. It was a well-known interpretation before the days of Athanasius, Eusebius and Arius. We can easily show that from the very earliest time this text had suffered violence, and violent men had perverted its meaning; but the most ill-proportioned things may often be set in surroundings where they can acquire a certain amount of dignity, and perhaps it was not wholly inept that the orthodox brained Arius (or tried to) with a missile taken from the armoury of the primitive Christians against the Jews. We will now show that this is the origin of the passage in question.

Bar Ṣalibi in his Testimonies[1] quotes as follows:

David said: Before the day-star I begat thee. And before the sun is his name and before the moon. Now explain to us, when was Israel born before the day-star, etc.

Here the controversialist has put together two passages in order to prove the pre-existence of the Son and His Eternity. At the same time he refutes the objector who says that this and similar things are said of Israel. The passages combined are from the 110th Psalm and from the 71st Psalm; the objection met is that some other person or persons than the Messiah are referred to. Now turn to Justin, *Dialogue with Trypho*, c. 63, c. 76 and c. 83, and you will find him harping on the same text and meeting a similar objection. "Your Rabbis," says Justin, "have dared to refer the Psalm (cx.) to Hezekiah and not to Christ." It follows that it was a controversial passage in Justin's day: you can hear the two disputants at their work. The Rabbis of whom Justin was speaking were replying to Messianic and Christian

[1] p. 28.

interpretations. In another passage (c. 76) Justin combines the
two passages from the Psalms as follows:

καὶ Δαβὶδ δὲ πρὸ ἡλίου καὶ σελήνης
ἐκ γαστρὸς γεννηθήσεσθαι αὐτὸν κατὰ
τὴν τοῦ πατρὸς βουλὴν ἐκήρυξε·

where it is easy to see the combined fragments of—

Before the day-star I begat thee from the womb;
Before the sun and before the moon His name shall abide.

The same blending of passages is found in c. 45, where
Justin speaks of Christ as being "before the day-star and the
moon."

But if we want further confirmation that the two passages
belong to a combination in a book of Testimonies, here it is in a
very primitive form from Gregory of Nyssa:

ἢ δῆλον πρὸς ὃν εἶπεν, ἐκ γαστρὸς πρὸ ἑωσφόρου ἐγέννησά σε· καὶ, πρὸ τοῦ
ἡλίου τὸ ὄνομα αὐτοῦ καὶ πρὸ τῆς σελήνης.

And here we have the primitive question "Of whom speaketh
the prophet this?" in a form which at once explains why later
editors proved that it was not Hezekiah, nor the ideal Israel.
It looks as if the form in Gregory of Nyssa were very near to the
original[1].

However, we have shown that the force of Athanasius' argument lay in the fact that he was quoting from the old Book of
Testimonies; for we not only find his proof-text in Justin and
elsewhere, but in two extant collections of such prophetic
evidence. And it will be seen that the Testimonies of Bar Ṣalibi
have much ancient material incorporated in them.

Perhaps enough has now been said to demonstrate the existence of the lost book whose influence the critics have been
suspecting.

As soon as we have accumulated enough evidence to enable
us to definitely state the existence of the primitive *Testimony
Book*, we can go on to use the recovered book for the criticism
of the early Patristic documents, and of the books of the New
Testament. We will first give a specimen of the way in which
the book can be traced in a sub-apostolic writer. Suppose, for
example, that we were studying the so-called second epistle of

---

[1] Cyprian, *Test.* I. 17, has merely Ps. cix. Ante luciferum genui te. Juravit
Dominus, etc.

Clement to the Corinthians. We find that as soon as the prologue is over, the second chapter plunges abruptly into a quotation from the beginning of Isaiah liv., "Rejoice, barren woman, that dost not bear," a passage with which we are familiar from its use in the Epistle to the Galatians. He proceeds to explain the application of the passage to the Church and the Synagogue, and continues thus: "In saying that the children of the desolate are more than of her that hath the husband, he was speaking to prove that our people seemed desolate and forsaken of God, whereas now we have believed and have become more than those who seemed to know God." Now turn to Justin's *First Apology*, c. 53, and you will find him making a similar statement from the same passage: "We know," he says, "that the Christians from among the Gentiles are more and truer than the Jews and the Samaritans." "It was prophesied that believers from among the Gentiles should be more in number than those who come from among the Jews and Samaritans. For it was said as follows: Rejoice, thou barren woman, etc....And that the converts from the Gentiles should be truer and trustier, we will declare by quoting the words of Isaiah the prophet." Then he proceeds to quote, not Isaiah, but Jeremiah (Jer. ix. 26), to the effect that Israel is uncircumcised in heart, the Gentiles are ceremonially uncircumcised. The same argument from prophecy appears in c. 31, where he tells us that it was foretold that the messengers of the Gospel should be sent to every race of men, and that the Gentiles should believe rather than the Jews. Now here we have all the features of the use of the *Testimony Book*. And when we turn to the *Testimonies* of Cyprian we find as follows:

Quod Ecclesia quae prius sterilis fuerat plures filios habitura esset ex gentibus, quam quot Synagoga ante habuisset.

This heading is followed by another:

Quod gentes magis in Christum crediturae essent.

Here we have the very points made by Justin and Ps.-Clement; the Gentiles more, truer and trustier; and the first proof-text is —

Apud Esaiam prophetam: Laetare, sterilis, etc.

It is needless to say more; the evidence is conclusive that the early book of Testimonies contained a section on the numerical and ethical superiority of Gentile Christians to Jews (or is it Judaeo-Christians?). And from the way in which the supposed

Clement plunges at once into the use of the book, we may be sure that it was familiar to him, and that it was not wholly unknown to his hearers.

The question that comes next is the possibility of our finding traces of the *Testimony Book* in the pages of the New Testament. The subject is suggested by the previous one which we were discussing from Ps.-Clement, where a passage is quoted which we also find used as a testimony in the Epistle to the Galatians (iv. 17). It is also suggested by the fact that we find an occasional failure in the references to the Old Testament on the side of authorship, as when Mark refers to Isaiah a prophecy of Malachi; and Matthew refers to Jeremiah a well-known passage about the potter's field. Besides these and similar errors we have curious features in the quotations of the Fourth Gospel which suggest composite quotation. We should also examine the sequence of the prophecies quoted in the New Testament in order to see whether they agree with the sequences in the *Testimony Book*, and we must try in such cases to find out which of the books has borrowed from the other.

For example, when Peter (1 Ep. ii. 6–8) says:

"Behold, I lay in Zion an elect corner-stone, etc.;
    He that believeth on Him shall not be confounded";

"The stone which the builders rejected is become the head of the corner, and a stone of stumbling and a rock of offence";

we have a sequence of quotations from Isa. xxviii. 16, Ps. cxviii. 22, Isa. viii. 14, the connexion between them being the word "Stone" as applied to Christ.

If we turn to Romans ix. 32, 33, we have the statement that

They stumbled at the stumbling stone, as it is written: Behold, I lay in Zion a stone of stumbling and a rock of offence, and he that believeth on Him shall not be confounded;

where the sequence is Isaiah viii. 14, Isaiah xxviii. 16, the two passages being neatly incorporated into an apparently single reference. The suggestion arises that the *Testimony Book* had made the conjunction; and in that case the headline must have been a statement that Christ is the Stumbling-stone, or something that would lead up to that. The anti-Judaic character of the quotation does not need to be stated. Did the Testimony books use this figure and the corresponding quotations? The answer is that it would take a whole chapter to illustrate the way in which the earliest of the Fathers harp upon the statement that Christ is called the Stone in the Scriptures. When we turn to Cyprian's *Testimonia* (II. 16) we find a section headed—

Quod idem et lapis dictus sit

followed by a section (II. 17)—

Quod deinde idem lapis mons fieret et impleret totam terram.

The first section begins with the first passage from Isaiah as in 1 Peter, and goes on to Psalm cxviii., but does not incorporate the second passage of Isaiah. The same references with the same omission will be found in Gregory of Nyssa[1]. The inference is that the treatment in Cyprian is conventional, and goes back to an early original. The verification of this is in Justin's *Dialogue with Trypho*, where Justin returns again and again to the statement that Christ is the Stone of the Old Testament, *e.g.*:

c. 34. I am going to show you from all the Scriptures that Christ is King and Lord and Priest and God and angel and man and general and *stone*, and the child that is born, and that he comes first to suffer (παθητός) and then returns, etc.

Amongst the proofs which Justin brings will be found agreements with Cyprian that Christ is the Stone which Jacob anointed at Bethel, etc. But, as I have said, it would make a long chapter to trace the doctrine that Christ is the Stone[2]. The history of the doctrine begins with the Lord's own use of the passage from the Psalm as an anti-Judaic testimony and was carried on and marvellously developed for two hundred years. It was certainly a leading point in the *Testimony Book*.

We ought also to examine whether there are in the New Testament traces of the matter and manner of the controversialist, as we find him in our study of anti-Judaism elsewhere. A simple instance will show what we mean.

In Acts xxvi. 23, Paul's speech before Agrippa contains the following statement; first, that he says nothing outside of what the prophets and Moses have said; second, he indicates in the following curious expression the matters to be discussed:

εἰ παθητὸς ὁ χριστός, εἰ πρῶτος ἐξ ἀναστάσεως νεκρῶν φῶς μέλλει καταγγέλλειν τῷ τε λαῷ καὶ τοῖς ἔθνεσιν.

No one, as far as I know, has succeeded in translating this sentence[3].

---

[1] Zacagni, p. 312.   [2] For Justin, *Dial.*, see further 70, 76, 86, 100.

[3] The R.V. margin comes nearest to it, with the suggestion "Whether" for εἰ.

It is clearly interrogative: "Does the Messiah suffer, and does he first rise from the dead, etc.?" The words are headlines of Testimonies, awkwardly incorporated in the text, and are betrayed as such by the previous references to the prophets and Moses, who are to answer the questions. And a reference to the previous quotation which we took from Justin, as to the things which he was going to prove from the Scriptures (in particular that Christ was the Stone), will show that he also proposed to demonstrate that Christ was $\pi a\theta\eta\tau\acute{o}s$. It is the same term as in the Acts, and means that the Messiah must suffer ($\acute{e}\delta\epsilon\iota$ $\pi a\theta\epsilon\hat{\iota}\nu$)[1].

We suggest, therefore, that this passage of the Acts shows the influence of the *Testimony Book*.

---

[1] Not "is capable of suffering," as in R.V. margin.

CHAPTER II

It is becoming increasingly clear that the *Testimony Book* is earlier in date than some of the earliest books of the New Testament; and that it is not mere oral Testimony that is involved is also clear from the antiquity and wide diffusion of errors which can only have arisen in a written book. So we continue our search for prophetic Testimonies in the pages of the New Testament, of the kind which we have been studying. We will presently devote a special section to the perplexing passage in Matt. xxvii. 9 where a sentence is referred to Jeremy the prophet that apparently should have been referred to Zechariah. If, as we suppose, the mistake is due to the transcriber of a book of prophetic proofs, it is clear that the antiquity of such a book must be considered as established, for it lay before the first Evangelist in such a form as was already showing some signs of transcriptional confusion.

Setting Matthew on one side for the present, we may argue the antiquity of the *Testimony Book* even more forcibly by reference to the opening verses of Mark. Every student knows that the second verse of the Gospel has been replaced by modern editors in the form

> As it is written in the prophet Isaiah,

in place of the conventional

> As it is written in the prophets.

Inasmuch as the words which follow are not from Isaiah, but from Malachi, it might seem that textual criticism had landed us and the Evangelist in a definite and undeniable contradiction. As the passage in Malachi

> Behold, I send my messenger, etc. Mal. iii. 1,

is immediately followed by

> The voice of one crying in the wilderness. Is. xl. 3,

the verdict of common sense would be that the received text is right, and the earliest codices of the New Testament are wrong. Criticism has, however, sometimes the right of way against common sense. In this particular instance the erroneous reference to Isaiah has clearly arisen in the *Testimony Book*, or in the use of it. Either the title of a quotation has slipped (a form of error of which we shall have abundant illustration), or the evangelist himself has let his eye wander from one marginal ascription to another in the sequence

> *Malachi.*   Behold, I send my messenger.
> *Isaiah.*   The voice of one crying.

The revised text is therefore wrong in fact but right in tradition; it was certain to be corrected at an early date, though it is the primitive text, and the obvious way to correct it is to write "in the prophets" in place of "in Isaiah the prophet."

The wrong text is, then, the primitive form, and it was probably a wrong text in the *Testimony Book* before it became a wrong text in Mark. The antiquity of the matter with which we are dealing is apparent.

There is another interesting point which comes up in connexion with this passage. The persistence of an error when once it has got into circulation is one of the surprising features in this kind of work. We have already had reason to show cases of such persistence in Justin, Irenaeus, Athanasius. A false ascription once made will be copied by the leading Fathers with a dog-like fidelity which shows that they were predisposed to believe that whatever was written ought to stand.

Now we shall presently be showing the influence of the *Testimony Book* upon an Arabic Christian writer against the Mohammedans, who uses the method of previous Christian writers against the Jews. It is a book which Mrs Gibson found on Mount Sinai and which she entitled a *Tract on the Triune Nature of God.* In this tract we shall show that the writer introduced one of his collected Testimonies from the prophets as follows:

God said *by the tongue of Isaiah* the prophet about the Christ and about John the son of Zacharia: I will send my messenger, etc. Mal. iii. 1.

Here we have the very same sequence as in Mark's opening verses. If it were likely that the anti-Moslem writer was quoting the Gospel of Mark, we should put him in evidence for the reading

of the oldest MSS.　It appears however from a study of his book
that he is retailing a collection of prophetical Testimonies, and we
conclude that the very same error which was in Mark's *Testimony
Book* passed into the East, and was found in the *Testimony Book*
of an anonymous Christian writer who wished to treat the Mohammedans in the same way that his predecessors had dealt with
the Jews.

The error, therefore, is pre-Marcan as well as Marcan.

We have thus made it clear that the *Testimony Book* antedates
the four Gospels, since it is earlier than the earliest of the four.

We have now, with a good degree of probability, established
by the examination of special cases the priority of the *Testimony
Book* to Matthew, Mark, Acts, 1 Peter and Romans: and we
may lawfully use our hypothesis in other passages of the same
writers and in other books of the New Testament, in order to
elucidate the meaning of the Scripture: and we may use our new
instrument with the greater confidence if the book to which we
apply it is anti-Judaic in character.　Of all the New Testament
books the Epistle to the Galatians is the most anti-Judaic and
perhaps the earliest.　Nearest to it in date we may put the
Epistle to the Romans; this Epistle becomes anti-Judaic in the
ninth chapter, where we have already detected the sequence of
Testimonies which prove that Christ is the Stone spoken of by
the prophets.　Is there any similar trace of conventional anti-
Judaic matter in Galatians?

We turn to Gal. iv. 27, where we read:

Rejoice, O barren, thou that bearest not:
Break forth and shout, thou that dost not travail with child:
For more are the children of the desolate, than the children of the married
　　wife.

It is not sufficient to annotate one's margin here with a reference
to Is. liv. 1: for we recall that one of the things that have to be
proved in the Cyprianic tradition is that a new race has come,
more faithful to God than the Jews and more numerous.　Suppose
we look at Cyprian's tradition as it occurs in Bk I. 19, 20.　We have

19.　*Quod duo populi praedicti sint, maior et minor ; id est vetus Iudaeorum
et novus qui esset ex nobis futurus.*

In Genesi: Et dicit Dominus Rebeccae: duae gentes in utero sunt et
duo populi de ventre tuo dividentur, et populus populum superabit, et maior
serviet minori.

Item apud Osee prophetam: Vocabo non-populum meum populum-meum, et non-dilectum dilectum: erit enim, quo loco dicetur non-populus meus, illo loco vocabuntur filii Dei vivi.

20.   *Quod Ecclesia quae prius sterilis fuerat plures filios habitura esset ex gentibus, quam quot Synagoga ante habuisset.*

Apud Esaiam prophetam: Laetare, sterilis, etc.

These two doctrines, the doctrine of the two peoples, and the doctrine of the moral and numerical superiority of the Gentiles to the Jews (or of Gentile Christians to Jewish Christians), occupy an important place in the arguments of the sub-apostolic Fathers. A single instance may be given in illustration of this. We will examine more in detail the passage which we quoted above from the *First Apology* of Justin Martyr and the fifty-third chapter; we find the following argument, which is expressly said to be taken *from prophetical Testimonies*:

I have *many other prophecies* to relate to you but at present I forbear, thinking the passages already quoted sufficient,......For how should we ever have come to believe in a crucified man, that he is the First-Born of God, and is to carry out the judgment of the whole human race, if we had not found, before his coming in human form, *such testimonies declared concerning him* and such as we see to have actually occurred, viz.: the desolation of the Jews' land, and men of every race, persuaded through the teaching of his apostles, to abandon the ancient customs of their life in error, seeing, as they did, that we had become, as Gentile Christians, *more numerous and more true* than those who belonged to the Jews and the Samaritans?......for it had been foretold that the believers among the Gentiles would be *more numerous* than those from the Jews and Samaritans, and we will repeat the prophecies to that effect.   It was said as follows:

Rejoice, thou barren one, etc.

(As to the Jews), who wills can see that their land is desolate and burned with fire, and remains a waste.   And to show you that the Gentiles were known beforehand as being *more true and more faithful*, we will relate to you some words of the prophet Isaiah.

It is quite clear that Justin is here harping upon the doctrine of the *Book of Testimonies* as we have it in Cyprian: he is not quoting St Paul directly.   We must then either say that he is quoting St Paul indirectly, in which case the *Testimony Book* becomes a pendant to the Epistles, or else we must say that the anti-Judaic parts of Romans and Galatians agree with Justin Martyr in a common dependence upon a primitive collection of *Testimonies*, and it is evident that the latter is the true explanation in view of what we have already deduced as to the antiquity of

such collections. St Paul's expression, "As he saith also in Osee"
is the reflection of "Item apud Osee prophetam" in the *Testimonies*.
If at first sight it seems surprising to find it suggested that the
collection of proof-texts from the prophets antedates all our
canonical Christian literature, a little reflection will show that the
result might almost have been anticipated: for certainly the first
need of the "new people" was just such an attestation as prophecy
could afford, and there were quarters where no other evidence
would have been accepted as a substitute for it.

We shall, then, say that the *Testimony Book* is one of the
earliest Christian documents, and that the earliest books of the
New Testament must be interpreted in the light of such a document
as we have shown, by so many considerations, to exist. The
student will, on the margin of his New Testament, add against
Romans ix. 12 the note Cyp. *Test.* I. 19, against the passage from
Hosea in Romans ix. 25 the same note, and against the cento of
passages on the Stone in Rom. ix. 32, 33 the note Cyp. *Test.* II. 16.
He will also add in the Epistle to the Galatians, against Gal. iv. 27
the references to Cyp. *Test.* I. 20 and to Justin, 1 *Ap.* 53.

In making these references, however, it will be well to remember
that not everything which occurs in the Cyprianic or Justinian
Testimony Book goes back to the original form. Some sentences
belong to a later date than the destruction of Jerusalem. It
would be easy to show that there was a fluid element in the
tradition. New occasions brought new proofs of the reproba-
tion of the Jews, and closer study often compelled the early
Christian to admit that all his arrows had not reached their mark,
and could not do so. All that we have established is that there
was an early collection of prophetical Testimonies against the
Jews, that it was arranged under suitable headings, and that in
some form or other it is earlier than the books of the New Testament.

CHAPTER III

The previous investigations and arguments will have made it clear that the *Testimony Book* is an important factor in the criticism and interpretation of the New Testament. It comes in as a judge to decide for us between the contending readings in the first verse of Mark: should we read "in Isaiah the prophet" or "in the prophets"? The *Testimony Book* will tell how the variant arose, and which is the original reading. In the same way, when we ask what we ought to read in Matt. xxvii. 9, 10, should it be "Jeremy the prophet" or just "the prophet," or some other reading? the judge will sum up the case for us and announce the verdict. In the cases mentioned, the decision is given on evidence, and between disputants. There are, however, cases where the *Testimony Book* throws light on the text, where there is no evidence available for its reconstruction or correction, and at first sight, no suspicion of inaccuracy. We propose now to draw attention to such a case, and to make a conjectural emendation to which we shall be guided by the book of early Christian teaching that we have unearthed.

In studying the text of the first Epistle of Peter the conviction has been deepening for a long time that it contains a large number of residual errors, such as cannot be cured by the aid of manuscripts which are at present at our disposal. Perhaps this may be due, in part, to the antiquity of the document, of which we may say that, as a whole, it is one of the best attested compositions of the New Testament. But this presumed antiquity can hardly be a complete explanation of its errors, supposing, that is, that we agree that the text still needs mending. For, after all, the difference in the length of life between this composition and other similar compositions in the New Testament is still very small even if we were sagacious enough in our criticism to establish definitely a chronological order for the books and pamphlets and letters which make up the New Testament. And it is, therefore, wiser to say that if residual errors should be detected or suspected in one particular book or tract, the reason must lie in the palaeographical fortunes of the book itself, and in its pre-canonical life, before it came to be a part of a recognized collection and treated like the rest of the books of which the collection is composed.

In the present brief chapter we propose to discuss the original form and meaning of the closing words of 1 Peter ii. 8, which stand in our Authorized Version in the form "Whereunto also they were appointed"; the Revised Version does not suggest any change in the rendering of the original text εἰς ὃ καὶ ἐτέθησαν, nor does it decorate its margin with an alternative either to text or translation; from which it may be inferred that they had no fault to find either with the one or with the other. Whether they liked the doctrine, as in all probability the Revisers of 1611 did, will not, of course, appear, as we have no printed records of the proceedings in the Jerusalem Chamber. If they did not like it (and it is one of the strongest pieces of predestinarian doctrine in the New Testament), they had no way of expressing it, for no one has any right in editing a text, to say whether he likes the text when he has edited it, or, to put it more exactly, to edit the text because he likes it. We have no control over the thoughts or expressions of Peter and Paul because we may agree or disagree with them in the matter of the Freedom of the Will, for the Freedom of the Will in a critic or a translator is a very limited Free Will, inside the circle of Free Will generally and very near the centre. So we must be cautious in saying that the text is wrong, merely because we may not like the statement that the unbelievers stumble at the Stone of Offence *and were appointed so to do*. The harshness may be the inevitable concomitant of the writer's theology, and in that case, what right have we to suggest a change? On the other hand, it is not impossible that the harshness may be an importation or a misunderstanding, and if we can find any evidence that bears upon that point, it is not improper to produce it.

But, first of all, let us examine the passage at length to which the words under consideration are a pendant. It is well known that this famous statement about the place of the Stone rejected of the Builders in the Divine Architecture is one of the passages which are held to prove the dependence of Peter upon Paul. The argument is as follows: here in Peter we have the statement, "Behold, I lay in Zion a stone, elect, a corner-stone, a precious stone, and he that believeth in Him shall not be confounded. To you, then, that believe He is precious; but to the unbelieving, the stone which the builders rejected is become the head of the corner, and a stone of stumbling and a rock of offence; who stumble at the word, being disobedient; whereunto also they were appointed."

Now in this passage we have a combination of two passages from Isaiah with a passage from the Psalms, the latter being also quoted in the Gospel of Matthew (xxi. 42), the two passages being Isaiah xxviii. 16 and Isaiah viii. 14. And in the quotation from Isaiah xxviii. 16 the writer is not working, as we should expect, from the text of the LXX; if he had been, he would have begun his quotation with ἰδοὺ ἐμβάλλω εἰς τὰ θεμέλια Σιών instead of ἰδοὺ τίθημι ἐν Σιών to say nothing of some other changes; so we have here either an independent translation or a reformed rendering of the LXX by reference to the original Hebrew.

Then it is further noted that the same two passages of Isaiah are found combined in Romans ix. 32, 33; "they stumbled at the Stumbling Stone, even as it is written, Behold, I lay in Zion a stone of stumbling and a rock of offence, and he that believeth on Him shall not be ashamed," where we see the same modified rendering of Isaiah xxviii. 16. And from thence it has been inferred that Pauline material has been worked over by Peter, for which opinion confirmation has been suggested in other quarters.

The same divergence from the LXX to the Hebrew will be found in the other quotation from Isaiah (viii. 14), for here the LXX has wrongly οὐχ ὡς λίθου προσκόμματι συναντήσεσθε αὐτῷ οὐδὲ ὡς πέτρας πτώματι: and it is this repeated coincidence between Peter and Paul in the selection and use of material that furnishes the ground for a belief in a connexion between the two writers. Dr Hort states the case thus: "St Paul substitutes a literal rendering of the Hebrew and St Peter follows him."

But then Dr Hort goes further and points out that the single word σκανδάλου, as used in this connexion by St Paul and St Peter, pointed back to characteristic language of our Lord Himself, as well as of the Evangelists, on His being a "stumbling-block" to the Jews who refused Him; as St Paul elsewhere pronounced a crucified Christ to be to the Jews distinctly a "stumbling-block."

But if this idea of stumbling at the Stone of Scandal is so widely diffused in the Gospels and Epistles, the question arises in our minds as to whether the teaching is not a part of the earliest Christian tradition, and whether the agreement between the two Apostles cannot be explained by the use of this tradition, without the necessity of their quoting one another. The use of the same passages of Isaiah in the same translation, and that an independent translation, points at once to the use of a *Book of Testimonies* anti-Judaic in character; if we can show reason for such a hypothesis, we can liberate Peter from the control of Paul, at least as far as this passage is concerned, and make them independent channels for the propagation of a primitive Christian argument. Now it is well known from the surviving collections of Testimonies against the Jews, and from quotations which may fairly be traced to such collections, that one of the earliest arguments embodied in them was based upon the statement that Christ is in the Old Testament known as the Stone. To establish this at length would take far too much space, and I will only refer to the matter very briefly; if we look at Cyprian's *Testimonies* we shall find in the same book three sections devoted to the establishment of the following points:

(*a*) That Christ is called the Stone;

(*b*) That then the same Stone should become a mountain and fill the whole earth;

(*c*) That in the last times that mountain should be made manifest, on which the Gentiles should come and into which all the just should ascend.

The proof-texts in Cyprian are Isaiah xxviii. 16, followed by the passage from the Psalm (cxviii. 22). Cyprian does not, however, quote the second passage from Isaiah, and in the first passage he appears to follow the LXX rather than the Hebrew (or is it a Latin text based upon the LXX?); for he reads:

Apud Isaiam prophetam sic dicit Dominus: Ecce *ego immitto in fundamenta* Sion lapidem pretiosum, electum, summum angularem[1] honoratum: et qui crediderit in eum non confundetur. Item in Psalmo cxvii. (=cxviii.), etc.

---

[1] The two words *summum angularem* are a translation of ἀκρογωνιαῖον.

Cyprian may then be taken as evidence for (1) the doctrine that Christ is the Stone, and (2) for the line of proof; although it does not run back demonstrably into the ancestry of the Peter-Paul quotations. Still, the substance of the arguments against the Jews is there and we shall find presently the same variation in the Epistle of Barnabas. So we suggest that the agreement between Peter and Paul is due to the use of the *Book of Testimonies*. The following further passage from Dr Hort will now require modification (*Comm. in* 1 *Pet.* p. 116):

> It is morally certain that St Peter borrowed from St Paul those peculiarities in his mode of quoting the passage which he has in common with him; and hardly less so that St Paul was not following any antecedent version other than the LXX, but freely adapting the LXX itself. Neither he nor St Peter had occasion to cite the reference, twice repeated in the Hebrew and the LXX, to the laying of foundations.

The first sentence in this passage needs now the expansion "or quoted from some collection of prophetical testimonies available to them both."

And now I want to draw attention to a curious passage in the Epistle of Barnabas, where we shall again come across traces of a similar gnosis with some striking variations; the text is as follows:

καὶ πάλιν λέγει ὁ προφήτης, ἐπεὶ ὡς λίθος ἰσχυρὸς ἐτέθη εἰς συντριβήν· ἰδοὺ ἐμβαλῶ εἰς τὰ θεμέλια Σιὼν λίθον πολυτελῆ, ἐκλεκτόν, ἀκρογωνιαῖον, ἔντιμον· εἶτα τί λέγει; καὶ ὁ πιστεύων εἰς αὐτὸν ζήσεται εἰς τὸν αἰῶνα (Is. xxviii. 16). ἐπὶ λίθον οὖν ἡμῶν ἡ ἐλπίς; μὴ γένοιτο· ἀλλ' ἐπεὶ ἐν ἰσχύϊ τέθεικεν τὴν σάρκα αὐτοῦ ὁ κύριος· λέγει γάρ· καὶ ἔθηκέν με ὡς στερεὰν πέτραν (Is. l. 7). λέγει δὲ πάλιν ὁ προφήτης· λίθον ὃν ἀπεδοκίμασαν οἱ οἰκοδομοῦντες, οὗτος ἐγενήθη εἰς κεφαλὴν γωνίας (Ps. cxviii. 22) (cp. Barnab. c. vi).

The variations in the text are curious, and the argument obscure; but it will at once be noticed that Barnabas is quoting the same passages from Isaiah and the Psalms that we found in Cyprian and quoting Isaiah xxviii. 16 as Cyprian does from the LXX. There can, then, be no doubt that Barnabas is using familiar matter from the *Testimony Book*.

Upon looking more closely at his statement we find him saying that Christ was set as a strong Stone *for breaking* (εἰς συντριβήν); and here we have an echo of the other passage from Isaiah concerning the Stone of Stumbling and Rock of Offence. Accordingly, Funk adds a note on this clause to the effect that Barnabas here seems to have in mind Isaiah viii. 14 in the Hebrew text. If this be so, we have the same text in Barnabas

as in 1 Peter, and Barnabas becomes the connecting link between
Cyprian and Peter-Paul. In this respect, then, the reference to
Barnabas is important; but there is more to come from it. Not
only does he hold the doctrine that Christ in the Old Testament
is represented as Stone and Rock (λίθος and πέτρα) but he
plays on the word (which Peter and Paul employ in quoting from
Isaiah) in such a way as to suggest that he knew the other
rendering from the Hebrew, in spite of the fact that he quotes
the LXX. The proof of this lies in the Greek of Barnabas which
is before us:

ὡς λίθος ἰσχυρὸς ἐτέθη εἰς συντριβήν·
ἐν ἰσχΰι τέθεικεν τὴν σάρκα αὐτοῦ ὁ κύριος·
ἔθηκέν με ὡς στερεὰν πέτραν,

and the repetition suggests a knowledge of the text ἰδοὺ τίθημι
ἐν Σιών instead of ἰδοὺ ἐγὼ ἐμβαλῶ εἰς τὰ θεμέλια Σιών.
And the importance of this observation is that it at once suggests
to us, from the repeated statements about Christ, that the words
in 1 Peter, with which we started, refer to Christ and not to the
disobedient or unbelievers, and that the text should be corrected
from εἰς ὃ ἐτέθησαν to εἰς ὃ ἐτέθη.

When this is done the passage becomes quite clear, for just as
Peter takes up the various terms in Isaiah and comments on
them, playing on the word ἔντιμον by a following ἡ τιμή and
reflecting the λίθος ἐκλεκτός in γένος ἐκλεκτόν, so he carries
on the thought of the laying of the foundation stone ("Behold,
I lay, etc.") and sums up the results of the laying of the stone in
the words, "For which cause also the stone was laid" (εἰς ὃ καὶ
ἐτέθη). It is curious how near Dr Hort came to this explanation
of the obscure clause in Peter: he remarks as follows:

ἐτέθησαν, a somewhat vague word in itself, expresses simply the ordinance
of God, perhaps with the idea of place added, that is place in a far-reaching
order of things. *The coincidence with* ἰδοὺ τίθημι ἐν Σιὼν λίθον *in verse 6
can hardly be accidental.* (Italics ours.)

Certainly the coincidence is not accidental, and the reference
to Barnabas enables us, by a simple conjecture, to make it exact.
It is a case of deliberate repetition from the opening words of
the passage quoted and commented upon.

Assuming this to be correct the exegesis of the passage is much
simplified. As long as it was a case of the dependence of Peter
upon Paul's quotations, it was almost inevitable that his argument

should follow the Pauline direction. From this point of view, Dr Hort said very properly that "all attempts to explain away the statement (εἰς ὃ καὶ ἐτέθησαν) as if, *e.g.*, it meant only that they were appointed to this by the just and natural consequences of their own acts, are futile." When, however, we see that it is the Stone that is the ordinance of God, and not the stumblers, the statement which Dr Hort takes exception to ceases to cause perplexity, and exactly expresses St Peter's mind. Something of the same kind is true with regard to the following sentences:

> These four mysterious words become clearer when we carry them back to what is doubtless their real source, those three central chapters of Romans of which the apostasy of Israel is the fundamental theme.

The words are no longer unduly mysterious, and they are to be understood without any reference to St Paul. We do not, of course, forget that this still leaves St Paul's argument against the Jews, by way of prophetical Testimonies, to be dealt with, and it may be difficult to extract from them any interpretation that must not be described as Predestinarian. All that we have urged is that the difficult words in Peter are to be interpreted without aid from Paul and in a different sense. In conclusion we may remark that the corrections and interpretations here offered have come to us gradually; the recognition that we were dealing with extracts from the *Testimony Book* came first; but here one was held up by the fact that the agreement with Cyprian was inexact. After that we came to suspect the genuineness of ἐτέθησαν and made the necessary marginal correction; it was some time, however, before we saw that Barnabas had been on the same track, that he agreed with Cyprian on the one hand, and probably with Peter on the other, and that he furnished a remarkable confirmation to the emendation which we had made.

CHAPTER IV

A FURTHER NOTE ON *TESTIMONIES* IN BARNABAS

In the preceding discussion of certain obscure words in 1 Peter ii. 8, according to which it seemed at first sight as if those who stumbled at the Corner Stone and Rock of Offence did so by necessity and of Divine Appointment, we tried to show from a parallel passage in the Epistle of Barnabas that there was a slight error in the text of Peter, and that it was the Stone which was appointed of God, and not, in Peter's view, those who stumbled at it: and we do not doubt that there will be not a few reverent students of the New Testament who will say something of this emendation which corresponds in theological language to the Shakespearean terms "for this relief, much thanks!"

In the course of the argument to which we refer it is shown that Barnabas was under the influence of one of those early collections of proof-texts from the Prophets which we call "Books of Testimonies," more exactly described in early times as *Testimonies* (or Quotations) *against the Jews*. This observation is quite independent of the question whether the text of 1 Peter ii. 8 ought to be emended or not. It is deduced from a coincidence (or at least an overlapping) between the argument of Barnabas and that which is involved in Cyprian's *Testimonies against the Jews*. And if the argument is a valid one, it must clearly be carried further. The detection of the source employed by the Epistle of Barnabas, or of the method which he follows, must lead to results in the exegesis of that perplexing document, and in one case at least, as we shall show, to the rectification of its text.

Let us, then, in the first instance, confirm the correctness of our observation, made by the juxtaposition of a passage in Barnabas with a sequence in Cyprian's *Testimonies* by trying for parallels and coincidences in another quarter.

Suppose we turn to Hilgenfeld's edition of the Epistle of Barnabas, and examine the cases which he has collected of the employment of Barnabas by later writers. We shall find that he recognizes a number of loans from Barnabas in a book which is ascribed to Gregory of Nyssa, as follows:

Gregorius Nyssenus in libello ἐκλογαὶ πρὸς Ἰουδαίους, 7, 11, 12, tacite reddidit Barnabae ep. c. 12, p. 31, 1, 2, c. 9, p. 22, 13 sq., c. 2, p. 6, 14 sq.; cf. quae adnotavi, pp. 74, 79, 113.

To the three cases here specified as instances of borrowing from Barnabas on the part of Nyssen, he adds a note that Nyssen has also borrowed from Clement of Rome:

Addo, Gregorium Nyssenum (c. 16, p. 322) etiam Clementis Rom. ep. 1, c. 53, p. 59, 1–3 usum scripsisse: Μωϋσῆς· Ἔασόν με ἐξαλεῖψαι τὸν λαὸν τοῦτον, καὶ δώσω σοι ἔθνος μέγα καὶ πολὺ μᾶλλον τούτου. Cf. Exod. xxxii. 31, 33.

Now concerning these supposed loans on the part of Nyssen from Barnabas and from Clement of Rome, it is sufficient to remark that the book is expressly called "Selections of Testimonies against the Jews": with the single exception that Nyssen says he has added somewhat in regard to the doctrine of the Trinity; and this statement is borne out by the structure of the book: thus in the passage where the influence of Clement of Rome has been suggested, the sequence in Nyssen is as follows:

Of the Jews, he says[1]: You have profaned it.

David: Ask of me, and I will give thee the Gentiles for thy inheritance, and the uttermost parts of the earth for thy possession.

Moses: Suffer me to wipe out this people, and I will give thee a nation, great, and much more than this.

Esaias concerning the Jews: Hear the word of the Lord, ye children of Sodom, etc.

Evidently there is not the least reason to suppose that in making an argument of this kind against the Jews the Epistle of Clement of Rome has any place. If any priority is to be claimed, it is for the document used by Nyssen, which must have been public property and a storehouse of quotations beyond any single writing of an apostolic Father. Hilgenfeld is, then, wrong in his reference to Clement. If Clement varies from the current text of the LXX, and combines separate Scriptures together, this would be only one more argument for the use of a *Testimony Book* by him, and not conversely.

But if Hilgenfeld is wrong in his note on Clement, he is equally

[1] Greg. Nyss. *l.c.* p. 322.

wrong in his three references to Barnabas on the part of Gregory of Nyssa. In order that the argument may be clear and decisive we will examine the passages in debate with some care.

Barnabas denounces the Jewish sacrifices as follows[1]:

> To what purpose is the multitude of your sacrifices?...For who hath required these things at your hands?...your new moons and your sabbaths I cannot away with.

Then he adds *de suo*:

> These things, then, he has done away (κατήργησεν) in order that the new law of our Lord Jesus Christ, which is without any yoke of necessity, might not have its offering a man-made thing.

Then he quotes again[2]:

> Did I ever command your fathers when they came out of Egypt to offer to me? etc.

Now in this connexion observe that the quotation with which Barnabas begins is in Cyprian, *Test.* i. 16, and that the heading of the section in Cyprian is

> Quod sacrificium vetus evacuaretur et novum celebraretur,

and that another section near by has the heading

> Quod jugum vetus evacuaretur et jugum novum daretur.

Here, then, in the Cyprianic titles we have the motive for Barnabas's reference to *new law*, and *new yoke*, and to the *abolition* (κατήργησεν) of the old law and yoke. Clearly Barnabas is using the *Testimony Book*.

The passage which he quotes from Jeremiah appears in Nyssen in the following form:

> *Esaias.* Did I ever command your fathers? etc.,

and again

> To what purpose is the multitude of your sacrifices? etc.

Here the false reference to Isaiah in the first quotation is an anticipation of the quotation which is to follow: and the displacement of the title is one more proof that Nyssen is working, as he affirms, from a *Book of Testimonies*. There is, therefore, no reason whatever for the supposition that Nyssen is quoting from Barnabas, when both he and Barnabas are seen to be quoting independently from collections of prophecies.

---

[1] Is. i. 11–13.　　　　　　　　[2] Jer. vii. 22, 23.

Now let us turn to the passage from Barnabas (c. 9) in which the writer denounces circumcision. Barnabas begins by saying:

But the very circumcision on which they trust has been done away (κατήργηται): for he said that there should be brought about a circumcision which is not of the flesh...and he says to them: Thus saith the Lord your God (so I find it commanded), Do not sow among thorns, be circumcised to your Lord[1]; and what is it that he says? Be circumcised in your hard hearts, and do not any more stiffen your necks[2]. Take another passage: Behold! thus saith the Lord, all the Gentiles are uncircumcised in their bodies, but this people are uncircumcised in heart[3]. But you will say, "Yes, but the people of God was circumcised for a seal." Truly, but so is every Syrian and Arab and all the idol priests, but they do not on that account come within the covenant, etc.

Does that look like the use of a *Testimony Book*? First, we notice that Cyprian (*Test.* I. 7) has a special section to show that circumcision is abolished. The title of the section is

Quod circumcisio prima carnalis evacuata est et secunda spiritalis repromissa est.

Compare this with Barnabas's introductory remarks and the priority of the Cyprianic matter is evident. Cyprian begins his bunch of quotations as follows:

In the prophet Jeremiah: Thus saith the Lord to the men of Judah and to those who inhabit Jerusalem: *renovate inter vos novitatem* and sow not amongst thorns: circumcise ye to the Lord your God, and circumcise the foreskin of your heart, etc.

That is, Cyprian begins with the very same quotation as Barnabas.

But what of Nyssen? He, too, has a section on circumcision. After some preliminary matter on the new covenant, he says:

In reproof of the Jews he says: All the Gentiles are uncircumcised in flesh, but this people in heart. And again: Be circumcised in your heart and not in your flesh. And again: Νεώσατε ἑαυτοῖς νεώματα, and do not sow among thorns, but circumcise the hard part of your heart.

Then follows an argument as in Cyprian and Justin and elsewhere about the just men who were never circumcised, etc.

Why should we say here that Nyssen is quoting Barnabas? he is nearer to Cyprian than to Barnabas in some points: he is ostensibly quoting Testimonies, and what he is doing ostensibly, we have shown that Barnabas is also doing, obscurely. There is not the least need to forge a link between Barnabas and Nyssen in order to explain the phenomena.

[1] Jer. iv. 3.   [2] Deut. x. 16.   [3] Jer. ix. 25.

Our third instance is a curious passage in which Barnabas maintains that the Christ is not the son of David, but his Lord. It runs as follows:

Since they are for saying that the Christ is son of David, David himself prophesies, in fear and knowing well the error of the sinful men[1]: The Lord said unto my Lord, Sit on my right hand, till I make thy foes thy footstool. And again Esaias speaks on this wise[2]: The Lord said to the Christ my Lord, whose right hand I have taken hold of, for the nations to obey before thee, and I will break up the power of kings. See how David calls him Lord, and he does not call him son.

If we examine the sequence here, we see that the argument of the first quotation is broken by the second one. Barnabas has copied too far from his book of extracts and has to turn back to pick up the thread of his argument. But that the passage from Isaiah was before him may be seen by referring to Cyprian on the one hand, and to Gregory of Nyssa on the other. For the passage from Isaiah is one of Cyprian's proof-texts that the Jews are to be displaced by the Gentiles (*Test.* I. 21 Sic dicit Dominus Deus Christo meo domino: cujus tenui dextram, ut exaudiant eum gentes: fortitudinem regum disrumpam, etc.), and the two passages from the Psalms and Isaiah occur together in Nyssen in the following intimate nexus (p. 324):

Whereas David says: The Lord said unto my Lord, Sit on my right hand, etc., Esaias puts it more clearly, The Lord said unto my Christ Cyrus. But they affirm this to be spoken of Cyrus, king of the Persians: ridiculous! how can that agree with the rest of the passage, I have holden thy right hand, etc.?

We now see how Barnabas was carried too far in his quotation: the two passages were closely linked in the *Testimony Book*. Nyssen does not take his extracts from Barnabas, but from an earlier and more archaic source.

These instances, then, will suffice to show that Barnabas is constantly running on the lines of the old anti-Judaic propaganda. His anti-Judaism is not original with him: it is only accentuated. Almost all the Fathers are trained on the same model: but we shall not rightly understand either them or him, either their texts or the interpretation of them, unless we are thoroughly familiar with the making and propagation of these little books of early Christian doctrine.

Let us apply the foregoing investigation to a special passage.

[1] Ps. cix. 1.　　　　[2] Is. xiv. 1.

The thirteenth chapter of Barnabas is taken up with the doctrine of *Two Peoples*: it corresponds to a section in Cyprian (*Test.* I. 19) whose heading is as follows:

Quod duo populi praedicti sint, major et minor, id est, vetus Judaeorum et novus qui esset ex nobis futurus.

Cyprian begins with the story of Rebecca and her approaching twin-birth, and the doctrine that the elder shall serve the younger. So does Barnabas who expands the theme. When Barnabas has satisfactorily shown that the Gentiles are the heirs of the covenant and its promises, he concludes the section with the following obscure passage: which we must give in the Greek:

εἰ οὖν ἔτι καὶ διὰ τοῦ Ἀβραὰμ ἐμνήσθη, ἀπέχομεν τὸ τέλειον τῆς γνώσεως ἡμῶν. τί οὖν λέγει τῷ Ἀβραάμ, ὅτι μόνος πιστεύσας ἐτέθη εἰς δικαιοσύνην; Ἰδοὺ τέθεικά σε, Ἀβραάμ, πατέρα ἐθνῶν τῶν πιστευόντων δι᾽ ἀκροβυστίας τῷ Θεῷ.

As we have said, there is something obscure about this: it runs as follows:

Our argument and our teaching will be complete if we can show that by Abraham mention was made.

Clearly something has dropped here, and a reference to what follows shows that the Gentiles have disappeared, the new people about whom he is arguing, for Abraham is the father of the faithful Gentiles. Suppose, then, we restore ἔθνη before ἐμνήσθη. Now let us look at the critical apparatus. *Three MSS. of secondary rank read ἐθνήσθη*! The genesis of the error is now obvious: the eye of an early scribe wandered from ΕΘΝΗ to ΕΜΝΗ, and thus an impossible reading arose. This has been corrected by the first-rank MSS. and versions by removing a faulty letter, but without restoring the dropped letters. Amongst these first-rank MSS. is the Codex Sinaiticus. The later MSS. are actually nearer to the truth at all events; by this time we have got the right text if we get it out of secondary MSS. on the one hand, and, on the other hand, out of a consideration of what the early *Book of Testimonies* was trying to prove. The argument now is that "our doctrine will be complete (as regards the supremacy of the Gentiles), if we can show that Gentiles are mentioned by Abraham. Does not the Scripture say, 'I have made thee a father to Gentiles' who believe, even though they lack the outward sign of the covenant of promise?"

CHAPTER V

TESTIMONIES AGAINST THE MOHAMMEDANS

The proofs of the antiquity and wide diffusion of the *Testimony Book* are already before us. Both in Latin and in Greek we have the evidence of some of the earliest and most influential writers. They come from Palestine, Rome, Asia Minor, Alexandria, Southern Gaul and North Africa. Such diffusion and such antiquity are the final proofs of our thesis of an Apostolic *Testimony Book*.

It remains, however, that we show that the literary phenomena to which we draw attention are not limited to the Greek and Latin Churches. We shall be able to detect the same propaganda, with similar documents, in the far East. This we shall do in two ways; one of which consists in the actual reproduction of a Syriac book of *Testimonies*, and the other in the analysis of a controversial work against the Moslems, in which the method of the earlier propaganda against the Jews has been deliberately imitated. From these two pieces of evidence, the Syriac and the Arabic texts, we shall sufficiently be able to show that the *Testimony Book* was not confined to the western side of the Euphrates. Our observations on the use of Testimonies against the Mohammedans were first published in the *American Journal of Theology* (Jan. 1901, pp. 75–86) as a review of a work which Mrs Gibson had recently published. This review is reproduced in the chapter that follows:

A Tract on the Triune Nature of God.

In a recently published number of the *Studia Sinaitica*[1] Mrs Gibson has edited and translated an Arabic discourse, in which a Christian writer attempts the conversion of his Moslem neigh-

[1] *Studia Sinaitica*, vii. An Arabic Version of the Acts of the Apostles and the seven Catholic Epistles from an eighth or ninth century ms. in the Convent of St Katherine on Mount Sinai, with a treatise on the Triune Nature of God, and translation from the same Codex. Edited by Margaret D. Gibson, M.R.A.S. Cambridge: University Press, 1898.

bours. The discourse is not quite complete, apparently through some fault of the copyist, and the name given to it is not the best that could have been chosen; but it contains so many early and valuable traditions belonging to the Eastern Church as to arouse the wish that the editorial care had been a little more complete with regard to the text, and that it had been accompanied by a commentary. This does not mean that we are ungrateful to Mrs Gibson for laying her transcripts and photographs before us in a written form; she and her sister have brought so much good metal out of the gold mine on Mount Sinai that the whole of the critical world is deeply in their debt; and we are disposed to think that this contribution to Arabic theology is by no means undeserving of a place among their other and more renowned publications.

When we say that the title of the book is wrongly chosen, a reason must be given for the adverse criticism; and it lies in the following considerations. The writer is aiming at the conviction of the believers in Islam in the very same way that generations of Christian writers, from the earliest times of the faith, had been in the habit of dealing with the Jews. He has used the same arguments that are found in the early Apologies against the Jews, the Dialogues with the Jews, and the collections of Testimonies from the Scriptures against the Jews. No one who is acquainted with this class of literature will fail to recognize the *disjecta membra* of Justin and Ariston, of Irenaeus, Tertullian, and Cyprian, and a number of other writers between whom there is a nexus, as regards both the matter and the manner of their arguments. And for this reason the tract should be called, not a treatise *On the Triune Nature of God,* but simply *Contra Muhammedanos.* It is not a dialogue between Christian and Moslem, nor is it exactly a collection of *Testimonia* against the Moslem; but it is, as nearly as possible, a tract *against* them, which occasionally slips into apostrophe, thus bringing us near to dialogue, and which more often strays off into the discussion of a string of texts which evidently belong to collections of *Testimonia;* it cannot, however, be described as either Dialogue or Testimonies. Behind the writer we see the line of earlier scribes whose themes are inscribed *Contra Judaeos*: he has borrowed from them, used their method, and incorporated their quotations. We could conserve the older title, if it were not for the fact that the testimony of the Koran is appealed to as an authority comprising the older Scripture, and if the writer had not in many cases deliberately imitated the style of the Koran and used its perspicuous language. For example, he begins his discourse with an imitation of the Fatha, or opening chapter of the Koran, as the following sentences will show:

We ask thee, O God, by thy mercy and thy power, to *put us among those who know thy truth and follow thy will* and [fear] thy wrath and adore thy excellent names in thy sublime attributes. *Thou art the compassionate, the merciful.*

And a little lower down we have again the language of Islam:

Verily, there is no God before thee, and no God after thee. To thee shall we return.

And so in a number of cases the language of the Koran is deliberately employed; and we think this literary artifice has not only made the discourse more acceptable to Moslem ears, but that the combination of the language and ideas of one Bible with those of the other has often resulted in passages of considerable beauty. But this is only the outward form of the discourse; Mohammed himself does not appear to be mentioned, nor any Moslem peculiarities; in the view of the writer the Moslem is only a new kind of Jew, to be converted by the methods of argument which have been from the beginning.

The value, then, of the tract consists in the fact that it is a survival of anti-Judaic literature. Such literature began early in the Christian Church, in the nature of the case, and it lasted late; it was produced by some of the most intelligent and devoted of the early Christian believers, so that, even in relatively late reproductions, it contains many forms of theological statement and many biblical quotations, which are altogether modified in the later Catholic traditions. It would be a good thing if some scholar would make a complete corpus of the anti-Judaic literature; and if such a collection were to be made, the latest members of the collection would be found to be often in striking coincidence with the second-century writers who would stand at the head of the volume. The same rare and perplexing readings of the Septuagint which we find in Justin Martyr, such as that "the Lord reigned from the tree," and that his enemies "put the wood [of the cross] on his bread," would be found in a chain of later writers; and even where it has ceased to be possible for later writers or readers to verify the quotations, by an appeal to either the Hebrew or the Septuagint, the arguments based upon the supposed texts die away very slowly. Such a collection as that of which we speak has been enriched in recent times by Mr Conybeare's publication of the dialogues of Athanasius and Zacchaeus, and of Timothy and Aquila, both of which are probably descendants of the lost second-century dialogue between Jason and Papiscus[1]; by a somewhat similar tract published by Professor McGiffert, called a *Dialogue between a Christian and a Jew*; and it is now further augmented by this tract of Mrs Gibson's. We are going to show some instances of the dependence of this new tract on the earlier Syriac and Greek literature; but we have not succeeded in identifying the writer of the tract so as to assign him his historical place among the defenders of the faith.

We shall show the dependence of the Arabic text upon earlier traditions, both in Greek and Syriac, by considering:

(*a*)   That the writer uses the same prophetic proofs as the early anti-Judaic apologists.

(*b*)   That he uses them in the same literary manner, by a method of mixed quotation and question, of which we shall give illustrations.

(*c*)   That there are traces of remarkable early readings in his biblical text, as well as of rare apocryphal allusions, most of which are explained by the existence of similar matter in the earlier anti-Judaic propaganda of the Church.

To begin with, then, the main body of prophetic proofs is the same as we find in early Christian writers, whether they are writers of dialogue, like Justin, or retailers of prophetical gnosis, like Irenaeus and Cyprian.

The writer of the tract begins his argument with the first chapter of Genesis, where he proposes to find the Father, the Word, and the Spirit; the Spirit being spoken of in the opening sentences concerning the ordering of chaos, the Son or Word being proved by a targumistic interpretation that "God said *by his Word*, Let there be light," and the whole Trinity being involved in the sentence, "Let *us* make man in our image." Now,

---

[1] See also Goodspeed, "Pappiscus and Philo," *American Journal of Theology*, October, 1900, pp. 796–802.

the antiquity of this method of reasoning is sufficiently obvious. The Targumist's explanation of the Word by which God spoke is not a product of the time of the rise of Islam; and the proof-text, "Let us make," etc., belongs to a very early stratum of anti-Judaic apology.

Turn, for example, to the dialogue of Athanasius and Zacchaeus, and you will find that Athanasius begins to reason with Zacchaeus from the first chapter of Genesis, draws his attention to the verse, "Let us make," etc., and then asks: "To whom did God say this?" Or, if you turn to Justin's *Dialogue with Trypho,* chap. 62, you will find the same verse used to prove that at least two persons are involved in the expression, and that one of these was the Word or Wisdom of God. Thus the prophetic passages selected by the Arabic writer can be seen to be a part of a gnosis that is almost as old as the Gospel itself.

Sometimes he quotes quite a block of prophetical Testimonies, as if he were working directly from a collection already in existence. For instance, when he wishes to prove that the Son of God descended for the salvation of the world, he reasons as follows:

One of the prophets said: "Lord, bend the heavens and come down to us" (Isa. lxiv. 1). One said: "O thou that sittest upon the cherubim, show thyself to us, stir up thy might, and come for our salvation" (Ps. lxxx. 1). And one of them said: "There is no intercessor and no king, but the Lord will come and save us." Another prophesied, saying: "The Lord sent his word and healed us from our toil and saved us" (Ps. cvii. 20). Another prophesied, saying openly: "He shall come and shall not tarry" (Hab. ii. 3). The prophet David prophesied, saying: "Blessed be he that cometh in the name of the Lord: God is the Lord and he hath appeared unto us" (Ps. cxviii. 26, 27). He said also: "The Lord shall come and shall not keep silence; fire shall devour before him, and it shall be very tempestuous round about him" (Ps. l. 3).

Now, these proofs of the coming and descending of God the Word are marked by curious features which reappear in the early Christian teaching at all points. They evidently form a part of an accepted tradition, and probably of a complete collection. One of the most curious is the proof of Christ's coming by means of the text: "He sent his word and healed us from our toil." When we turn to Cyprian's *Testimonia* (II. 3) under the heading, "Quod Christus idem sit sermo Dei," we find among the proofs:

Item in Psalmo cvi. (=cvii.) "misit verbum suum et curavit eos."

When we turn to Ephrem's commentary on the Diatessaron (p. 121), we find as follows:

Et quum Deus eis salvatorem misisset, qui eos educeret, ille immundus aufugit et sanati sunt. Misit verbum suum et sanavit et liberavit eos a perditione[1].

So in Gregory of Nyssa, *Adv. Judaeos*, we have in the opening chapter as a proof of the Being of God the Word the following verse:

ἀπέστειλε τὸν λόγον αὐτοῦ, καὶ ἰάσατο αὐτοὺς καὶ ἐρρύσατο αὐτοὺς ἐκ τῶν διαφθορῶν αὐτῶν.

Even more remarkable is the passage that precedes it in the Arabic text. Whence does this passage come which tells us that "there is no intercessor and no king, but the Lord will come and save us"? Observe that "king" is here a misreading for "angel," either in the Arabic or an underlying Syriac, and then turn to the Septuagint of Isa. lxiii. 9, "Non senior neque angelus, sed ipse Dominus liberabit." We give the Latin as it is quoted in Cyprian's *Testimonia*, II. 3. The quotation occurs again on p. 17 of the Arabic tract in the following form:

Isaiah said also by the Holy Ghost, "There is no angel and no intercessor, but the Lord will come and save us."

Here the text has rightly "angel," but the incorrect "intercessor" still remains in place of "presbyter," of which it can, perhaps, be shown to be a corruption or equivalent. Mrs Gibson suggests that the passage is Isa. lix. 16, but a little examination will show that it is Isa. lxiii. 9; the verse is a favourite one with the early Fathers. For instance, when Irenaeus (ed. Massuet, p. 214) gives the prophetic gnosis of the Incarnation, he begins with the words:

Rursus, quoniam neque homo tantum erit, qui salvabit nos, neque sine carne, sine carne enim angeli sunt, praedicavit enim, dicens: *Neque senior, neque angelus, sed ipse Dominus salvabit eos, quoniam diligit eos, et parcet eis, ipse liberabit eos.*

Grabe's note on this passage throws some light on the "intercessor" of the Arabic, for he says: "Vocem πρέσβυς hic non

---

[1] The form of the quotation, both here and in the Arabic tract, can be illustrated from the text of the Peshito, on which they may ultimately depend:

ܡ̇ܪܙ ܚܠܟܠܘ ܗ‍ܠܟܠܘ ܐܠܐ، ܗܩܝܘܒ ܐܠܐ، ܡܠ ܡܠ ܒܚܠܐܠ:

seniorem, sed *mediatorem*, vel *legatum*, significare, ex sequenti ἄγγελος colligo."

Let this, then, suffice to show the antiquity of the peculiar set of quotations in the Arabic tract. Almost all the prophetic gnosis contained in it is archaic. In the next place, observe that the method of using the gnosis is also primitive. If we turn back to the quotation from Gen. i. 14, "Let us make man in our image," we find Athanasius in the dialogue with Zacchaeus asking the question: "To whom did God say this?" Turning to Gregory of Nyssa, *Adv. Judaeos*, we find the quotation again accompanied by the question, τίς εἶπε καὶ τίς ἤκουσε; from which we begin to suspect that the method is a conventional one among those who use the prophetic gnosis; they make a quotation and then ask a question on it. For example, it is a favourite case to quote the account in the book of Genesis concerning the destruction of Sodom, "And the Lord rained fire and brimstone from the Lord," etc., and then to ask: "Which Lord rained fire from which Lord[1]?" These prophetic quotations and questions are characteristic of this branch of literature; and it is interesting to watch how faithfully the same method is followed in the Arabic tract. For example, in discussing the Messianic passage in Ps. lxxii. "His name shall be blessed for ever; His name endures before the sun and moon throughout all ages," the writer puts the question:

About whom among men did God's prophet prophesy, or, among the kings of the earth, whose name is blessed among the nations? or whose name endures before the sun and before the moon, save the Christ the Word and the Light of God?

The proof-text in the early gnosis that the Christ should heal all diseases is Isa. xxxv. 3, "Then the eyes of the blind shall be opened, and the ears of the deaf shall hear," etc., upon which our writer remarks:

When were weak hands and feeble knees strengthened, till our God came to us?...When did the eyes of the blind see, and the ears of the deaf hear, and the feet of the lame come on like a hart, and the tongues of the dumb speak plainly, save when the Christ appeared to us?

[1] The passage is a favourite one for the anti-Jewish polemist; it will be found discussed in Justin, ˜*Dial.*, 56, and the same passage, with the proper question attached, is in *Athanasius and Zacchaeus*, p. 12, ἆρα παρὰ ποίου κυρίου κύριος ὁ Θεὸς ἔβρεξε ἐπὶ Σόδομα καὶ Γόμορρα θεῖον καὶ πῦρ;

At the close of the printed tract we find the prophetic proof of the doctrine of baptism in the following words:

> God said by the tongue of Isaiah the prophet, Wash you, make you clean; put away your sins from before the Lord; and then the question is asked: "What bath or washing puts away the sins of men from before the Lord save the confession of sins and repentance toward God, and the immersion of baptism in the name of the Christ?"

It would be easy to furnish further parallels to this mode of composition out of the extant anti-Judaic literature. Let us now, having sufficiently demonstrated that the Arabic tract against the Moslems is a survival from a long line of similar tracts against the Jews, inquire whether there are traces of rare early readings in the quotations from the Scriptures, and whether there are apocryphal expansions and additions of the same. Perhaps the most striking passage for study is the following:

> Zechariah the prophet prophesied by the Holy Ghost, saying: Rejoice greatly, O daughter of Zion; shout, O daughter of Jerusalem. Behold! thy King cometh unto thee, riding upon an ass and her foal. The Christ came in, when he entered the Holy City, sitting upon an ass, on the day of the palm trees. The children of Israel met him with olive trees and palm branches, with their wives and children. The babes and sucklings adored him, saying: Hosanna to the Son of David: blessed is he who cometh King of Israel. The priests of the Jews said to the Christ: Hearest thou not what these say, doth not their saying exalt thee when they adore thee as God is adored? The Christ said to them: Have ye not read in the psalms of the prophet David what he said by the Holy Ghost, Out of the mouths of babes and sucklings thou hast foreordained thy praise? This is in the eighth psalm.

Examination of this passage shows that it is not a piece of original composition on the part of the writer of the tract, nor does the account come simply from the canonical gospels. We notice, in the first place, the peculiar statement that "the children of Israel met him"; then we are struck by the appearance of olive branches along with the conventional palm branches[1]; then we have the curious expansion that the people who met him were accompanied by their wives and children. Now turn to Mr Conybeare's edition of the *Dialogue of Timothy and Aquila*, p. 93, in which the same theme is handled; here we are told:

> ὅτ' ἂν ἀπάντησαν αὐτῷ οἱ παῖδες τῶν Ἑβραίων κράζοντες τὸ ὡσαννά, ἐν τῷ εἰσελθεῖν αὐτὸν εἰς τὸν ναόν, τότε ἐκύκλωσαν αὐτὸν οἱ ἀρχιερεῖς καὶ οἱ πρεσβύτεροι τοῦ λαοῦ λέγοντες, οὐκ ἀκούεις, τί οὗτοι σοῦ καταμαρτυροῦσιν ; ὁ δὲ

---

[1] We have the same conjunction in Chrys., *Comm. in Joann.* xii. 2 (Hom. 66): τὰ δὲ βαΐα τῶν φοινίκων καὶ τῶν ἐλαιῶν ἔλαβον.

Ἰησοῦς εἶπε· ναί· γέγραπται γὰρ ἐκ στόματος νηπίων καὶ θηλαζόντων κατηρτίσω αἶνον.

Mr Conybeare, in his "Introduction," p. xv, had drawn attention to the curious uncanonical elements in the biblical text as quoted by the author of *Timothy and Aquila,* and had furnished parallels to the παῖδες τῶν Ἑβραίων from the *Acts of Pilate,* where we find:

(*A.* I. 3) οἱ παῖδες τῶν Ἑβραίων κλάδους κατεῖχον ἐν ταῖς χερσὶν αὐτῶν, καὶ ἔκραζον.

(*A.* I. 4) οἱ παῖδες τῶν Ἑβραίων Ἑβραιστὶ ἔκραζον.

It seems, then, very probable that in the "children of Israel" of the Arabic tract, and in the "children of the Hebrews" of *Timothy and Aquila* and the *Acts of Pilate,* we have a trait from an uncanonical gospel.

But what of the branches of olive? In the same *Dialogue of Timothy and Aquila* we have on p. 71:

ὅτι δὲ τὰ νήπια, λέγω δὴ οἱ παῖδες τῶν Ἑβραίων, ἀπάντησιν αὐτῷ ἐποιήσαντο μετὰ κλάδων ἐλαιῶν λέγοντες τὸ ὡσαννά, Δαυὶδ λέγει ἐν τῷ ὀγδόῳ ψαλμῷ.

Here we have the *branches of olive* as in the Arabic tract, and even the apparently unimportant allusion to the psalm as the eighth psalm is paralleled by the Arabic writer, who says: "*This is in the eighth psalm.*" It appears, then, that our writer belongs to the same line of tradition which can be traced in *Timothy and Aquila,* and that there are features in his gospel which do not appear to be canonical and cannot be explained by the use of the harmonized gospels. Moreover, he is independent of *Timothy and Aquila,* in that he has a special proof that the babes and sucklings *adored the Christ*—a point to which he returns again and again. He also expands the question of the elders of the people (whom he calls *the priests of the Jews*), "Hearest thou not what these say?" by the words, "doth not their saying exalt thee when they adore thee as God is adored?"

It seems, then, that our tract furnishes fresh material for the study of the triumphal entry, and it may turn out that there is a variant tradition of that event, earlier than that found in the canonical gospels and independent of them.

We pass on to another point in which the traces of an earlier tradition may perhaps be found. It will be remembered that the commission of our Lord to His disciples is declared by a group of early writers, with some support from the Gospels and Acts, to have been given at the time of the Ascension. Thus the "western text" of the Acts opens with the statement concerning things which Jesus began to do and to teach:

On the day when he chose his disciples by the Holy Spirit and commanded them to preach the gospel [*Acta Apost. sec. formam Rom.*, ed. Blass].

Now, in the Arabic tract, p. 13, we find as follows:

When he said to the apostles *as he went up to heaven from the Mount of Olives* and commanded them to disperse themselves in all the world and preach about the kingdom of heaven and repentance in his name, the Christ said to them: "I send you this day as sheep amongst wolves, but tarry ye in the holy house until ye are clothed with power from heaven. I go to where I was, and I will send you the Paraclete, the Holy Ghost, the Righteous One, whom men cannot look on, him who will bring me to your remembrance and everything of which I have spoken to you. He will speak in your mouths, and ye shall be led before kings of the earth and rulers. Be not at all troubled about what ye shall speak, for the Spirit whom I shall send unto you, he shall speak in your mouths."

At first sight this seems a mere cento of recollections from Matt. x. 16; Luke xxiv. 49; John xiv. 17, 26; Matt. x. 18, etc. But even so, there are some touches of antiquity about the combined texts. We compare the instruction to tarry *in the holy house* with Luke xxiv. 53 (they were continually *in the temple*, blessing God). The expression seems earlier than the other two Lucan terms, "tarry in the city" and "do not depart from Jerusalem."

Then note the substitution of the term "kingdom of heaven" for "the gospel." We have the same substitution on p. 35, where the Christ said in the gospel to the apostles: "Go out into all the world, and proclaim *the kingdom of heaven* amongst the nations," etc. Here the quotation is not covered by the last verses of Mark; and the substitution of the earlier term should be remarked, for it agrees with Luke ix. 2 and other passages. It is quite within the bounds of possibility that the gospels known to our writer had independent readings, and perhaps some precanonical elements. The fact that the writer handles his biblical matter freely does not altogether explain the existence of peculiar phrases like those to which we have drawn attention. Some of his expressions may perhaps be traced to the use of peculiar or early types of canonical gospel without the introduction of such gospels as are definitely uncanonical. For example, in introducing one of his prophetic testimonies he says:

God said by the tongue of Isaiah the prophet about the Christ and about John the son of Zacharia: I will send my messenger, etc. [Mal. iii. 1].

Here the substitution of Isaiah for Malachi is an error of a type which is very common in collections of *Testimonia*, where the names attached to the extracts are frequently affected by original blunders as well as by faults of transcription; but since the same error is found in Mark i. 2, we have no need to go beyond the gospels for the explanation. Still the suggestion will present itself as to whether, after all, the original cause of the error may not lie in a false ascription in some collection of Testimonies, both as regards the Arabic writer and the Gospel of Mark. A similar error will be found on p. 28 in the quotation of the famous passage from Baruch iii. 35, 36: "He knew all the paths of knowledge and gave them to Jacob his servant and to Israel his saint. After this he looked upon the earth and mixed with the people." This passage is introduced by the words: "*Jeremiah* prophesied by the Holy Ghost." It is a very favourite quotation with the earlier anti-Judaics. We may compare Irenaeus, p. 254; *Altercatio Simonis*, I. 6; *Athanasius and Zacchaeus*, XXI. 24; *Timothy and Aquila*, p. 69, etc. It is interesting to observe that in the *Dialogue of Athanasius and Zacchaeus* the Jew protests against the ascription of the passage to Jeremiah, which is a good proof of the diffusion of the wrong ascription, and may also be taken as evidence of the antiquity of the sources of the Arabic tract, in which Jeremiah still reigns supreme.

Occasionally we find what appear to be apocryphal expansions to the gospel quoted. Thus on p. 27 we have:

> The Christ said to them: What is it right to do on the sabbath day, to do good, or evil? that life should be saved or destroyed? [Mark iii. 4; Luke vi. 9.] They said: Nay, let us do good on the sabbath and let life be saved. The Christ said to them: Ye speak truly. Then he said to him that had the withered hand, etc.

It is difficult to believe that this is evolved by mere expansion from the account in the sixth chapter of Luke. Certainly it could not have been derived from the Western text of Luke (or the ordinary text of Mark), which makes Christ look round him in anger, instead of speaking in approbation. Nor could it come from Mark, chap. iii., where the Pharisees "hold their peace" at the question. Nor does it consist with the canonical text at all, in any recension, which says that the Pharisees were "filled with madness," whereas our writer will have it that "the children of Israel who saw it were amazed, and they knew that no man can

work the work of the Christ, and many people believed on him."
It may, therefore, be suggested that the account of this miracle
used by the Arabic writer has in it an extra-canonical element,
which may turn out to be ancient and valuable.

We will conclude our examination as to the existence of
apocryphal or uncanonical elements in the tract by turning to
the case in which the writer is definitely convicted of the use of
an uncanonical apocryphal gospel. On p. 12 we find as follows:

> The Christ said to the children of Israel: If ye believe not in me, believe
> in my work which I do [John x. 38]. The Christ created, and no one can
> create but God[1]. You will find in the Koran: "And he spake and created
> from clay like the form of a bird, and breathed into it, and lo! it became a
> bird by the permission of God."

The extract is from the third Sura of the Koran, and the complete
text is as follows:

> The angel saith: So God createth that which he pleaseth; when he
> decreeth a thing, he only saith unto it, Be, and it is. God shall teach him
> [Jesus] the Scripture and the wisdom and the law and the gospel; and shall
> appoint him his apostle to the children of Israel; and he shall say: Verily I
> come unto you with a sign from your Lord, for I will make before you, of
> clay, as it were the figure of a bird, and I will breathe thereon, and it shall
> become a bird, by the permission of God: and I will heal him that hath been
> blind from his birth, etc.

Here the Koran, as is well known, is drawing upon the apocryphal
gospels of the infancy and boyhood of Jesus. What is interesting
is that the motive for the story of the creation of the sparrows is
betrayed by our Arabic writer, viz., that *Christ was proved thereby
to be the Creator*; when, therefore, he told the sparrows to fly
away, he was doing what the Creator did in Gen., chap. i. when
he said, "Let fowl fly on the face of heaven"; and when he told
the birds to remember him, it is not unreasonable to read into the
words, as Dr Taylor does, an allusion to Eccles. xii. 1, "Remember
thy Creator." The motive is obscured in the apocryphal gospels,
as they have come down to us, by the suggestion that Jesus did
the deed of power *on the sabbath*, but Mohammed seems to be
dealing with the question of an actual creation by Jesus, for he
explains that it was done by express permission of God, to whom
it belongs to say to a thing, "Be," and it is. If this be the right
explanation of the genesis of the legend of the sparrows, then we

---

[1] The passage from John is quoted by Cyprian, *Test.* ii. 6 under the heading
Quod Deus Christus.

should head the story with the statement of our tract that "the Christ created, and no one creates but God."

But now enough has been said to prove our first statement as to the important elements that are contained in the tract to which we have been referring. It need scarcely be said that the discussion of the prophetic gnosis involved in its pages might be carried much farther, and that it is susceptible of much more extended illustration. But for the present let it suffice to have demonstrated the affinity of the tract with the earlier anti-Judaic literature, and to have shown that the Eastern Church stood toward the Moslem in much the same position that they had occupied from the beginning toward the men of the Synagogue.

CHAPTER VI

"SPOKEN BY JEREMY THE PROPHET"

After writing the review which is reproduced in the previous chapter, I was able in the *Expositor* for Sept. 1905 to work out at some length the problem of the false ascription in the Gospel of Matthew (xxvii. 9) of a series of prophecies which were supposed to refer to Judas the traitor, and were definitely ascribed to Jeremiah.

This article I have here reproduced with one or two slight changes, to avoid undue repetition of matters dealt with in the previous chapters.

An ancient controversy, of which traces may be found from early ages of the Christian Church down to recent time, has recently been revived amongst us by the instrumentality of a leading newspaper. I refer to the dispute over the right reading or correct interpretation of a notable passage in the Gospel of Matthew (Matt. xxvii. 9) relating to the purchase of the Field of Blood by Judas the Traitor, which is said to have been foretold in ancient prophecy in the following words:

> Then was fulfilled that which was spoken by Jeremy the prophet, saying: And I took the thirty pieces of silver, the price of the priced one whom they priced from the children of Israel, and gave them for the potter's field, as the Lord enjoined upon me.

The controversy is, of course, as to how the Evangelist, supposed inerrant, could have ascribed to Jeremiah a prophecy of which the nearest parallel is in Zechariah (Zech. xi. 12) (though even in the supposed parallel the agreement between the book and its quotation is not very obvious).

The occasion of the revival of the controversy was as follows: Dr Armitage Robinson had delivered a series of Saturday afternoon lectures in Westminster Abbey, and in trying to restate the doctrine of inspiration, so as not to involve inerrancy, he alluded to this passage and pointed out that there had always been leading Christian teachers who had taken the liberty of disbelieving statements made in the Bible, and, having carefully ensconced himself under the wings of Origen or of Augustine, he announced from his selected shelter that St Matthew could not have been right in referring the prophecy in question to Jeremiah.

Up to this point there was nothing very novel in the treatment of the subject: it was neither epoch-making nor earthquake-making; the preacher merely stated what every textual critic of any historical standing had maintained, that the right reading in the passage of Matthew was "Jeremiah," and that the generally accepted conclusion was that the first Evangelist had made an incorrect reference. There can be no doubt that both of these critical statements would commonly pass unnoticed. It was singular that they should have been so vigorously challenged, first, under the head of the text; second, under that of the deduction drawn from it. Mrs Lewis wrote to the *Times* to point out that in her Old Syriac Gospels there was no mention of any prophet at all, and that this omission on the part of a very early Eastern version was supported by early Greek and Latin evidence. And it was inferred that the blunder might be removed from the shoulders of St Matthew and laid upon one of his earlier transcribers or editors who was not so much bound by the law of inerrancy as St Matthew was supposed to have been. Mrs Lewis, accordingly, solved the problem by erasing the difficulty. In this she was merely doing again what the earliest critics of the New Testament had attempted. I suspect she is unduly in love with the inerrancy of the Bible, and perhaps like Tischendorf, whom in many ways she resembles, is a little prejudiced in favour of evidence which she herself has brought to light. It must, however, in fairness be stated that she did not appeal for a reversal of the verdicts of previous New Testament critics, without producing fresh evidence, and that evidence has an extraordinary weight of its own. I will not say that Tischendorf would have reversed his judgment under the new warnings from Mount Sinai, though perhaps he might have done so; we may feel sure, however, that it would not have made the slightest impression on Dr Hort. I only wish to point out that it does, in my own judgment, make a difference in the balancing of the evidence, to have such a heavy weight put into the scale from an unexpected quarter. And Mrs Lewis was quite justified in moving for a new trial, if she thought the matter had, up to the present, been, from a defect in the evidence, wrongly decided. My own view is that the text is right as it stands; a fresh reason for this opinion will come a little lower down.

Mrs Lewis was followed by Dr Waller, who accepted the reading "Jeremiah," and brought the Old Testament to book for having wrongly labelled a certain part of the prophecies which pass under the name of Zechariah. The credit of the New Testament was thus saved at the expense of the Old; both are inspired, this and that, but it is the other one that is wrong. We close the door upon the Higher Critics of the New Testament by throwing open the question of authorship in the Old Testament! Desperate men choose desperate remedies!

Dr Armitage Robinson referred to these criticisms when he published his lectures[1]; he added a note in which he stated the objections of his critical antagonists, without referring to them by name, and concluded by saying that "it is better, with Origen and Augustine, to admit the difficulty; and then we may try to learn its lesson." He did not tell us what the lesson was exactly, nor why it should take much trying to master it. It is at this point that I propose, uninvited, to come to his assistance.

It has been my habit, for some time past, to warn my students that the Christian literature does not necessarily begin with the New Testament, and certainly not with the Gospels; that there are traces of previous documentary matter on which the accepted and canonical New Testament depends; and that, until we have learnt to recognize and isolate these primitive deposits, we shall constantly be making mistakes in our interpretation of the New Testament and the Apostolic Fathers. And, in particular, I tell them that there are two lost documents of the early Christian propaganda, occurring in various forms, sufficiently alike to constitute a cycle or type, the traces of which are to be found constantly in the first period of the literature of the Church. Of these the first is the *Collection of the Sayings of Jesus*, the second is the *Book of Testimonies* from the Old Testament. The first of these underlies the Gospels, and is especially an instrument for the conversion of the Gentiles: the second is an instrument for the refutation of the Jews.

The *Book of Sayings* does not come before us at the present

[1] *Some Thoughts on Inspiration.* Longmans.

time, and I am aware that, in referring to it, I have the opposition of a number of leading scholars to the belief in its antiquity
and in the possibility of the recovery of any of its very early
forms. I am the less anxious to discuss the matter, as I hold it
to be, in one respect, a case of Time *versus* Tradition, and that,
when we have reduced our prejudices in favour of the antiquity
of the Gospels to more sober limits, we shall ultimately agree well
enough as to the *Book of Sayings* and its antiquity and value.
But the other matter is even more important and far-reaching,
and it colours the whole of the early Christian theology, as well as
some of the theology in our own day, which can be shown to be
derived, in an unbroken line, from early disputes between Jews
and Christians, in which the latter employ the Old Testament, or
rather, a series of selected passages from the Old Testament, to
establish the truth of the new revelation.

It is to such a hypothesis of a controversialists' *vade mecum*,
confirmed as it can easily be by a study of Apostolic and sub-
Apostolic literature (especially of such parts as would belong to
a *Corpus Anti-Judaicum*, if such a book were to be produced as
it certainly should be produced), that I am in the habit of referring
for the elucidation of recurrent textual phenomena which cannot
be wholly due to manuscript variations, and for the study of the
crystallization of the leading Christian doctrines.

It would be comparatively easy to show, though this is not
the place to do it, that such *Testimonies* as those I allude to were
classified into sections with titles, brief explanations, and frequent
insertions of questions and comments by the controversialist
editor. And it is often from the recurrence of such editorial
matter, especially where the editor makes mistakes in his references to authors or in his interpretations of them, that we are
able to detect the use of the *Book of Testimonies* and to isolate
the matter which succeeding writers have borrowed from it. But
even where there is no editorial matter, the existence of centos
from the Scriptures, combining passages in a set order and with
substantially the same variations and connecting links, will often
betray the use of the lost little book of which we are speaking.

It can be shown, moreover, that it was common to make a
brief reference to the author of the extract given, usually under
a very simple form, such as "David says in the Psalm," or "Moses
says"; and sometimes only the name "David" or "Moses," or

whoever it may be, is given for verification; and it need hardly be said that the *Book of Testimonies* was subject to all the errors that such collections commonly develop, that the names often dropped out, or were attached to the wrong passages. It would, I think, be possible to write quite an interesting article on the traces of such transcriptional errors in the early Christian literature.

The suggestion then arises (and it will be a startling one to those to whom the subject is altogether new) that the Gospel of Matthew has been using a *Book of Testimonies*, in which the history and tragic end of Judas was explained as a fulfilment of ancient prophecy, and that the mistake which has vexed so many righteous souls was not necessarily even an original one in the Gospel, but one which either existed in the *Book of Testimonies*, or was accidentally made by the Evangelist in using such a book. In the latter event, the matter is not original, though the erroneous use of the matter may be so described. In the former case the mistake, if it be one, is higher up, and the text of the Evangelist must be replaced by the text of his source.

Such, in brief, is the explanation which has been in circulation privately for some time, and it is quite possible that it has been publicly made elsewhere. I should not, however, in view of the lack of direct support of the hypothesis, have drawn attention to it, if it had not been that the requisite verification recently turned up in a Syriac writer, to whom I shall presently allude. And even in this case I should probably have kept the verification to myself, until I was able to publish [the present] dissertation upon the *Book of Testimonies*, if it had not been that a discussion had been going on in the public press on the subject, and it seemed hardly fair to withhold an important and perhaps a decisive piece of evidence, which is at least as weighty in such a connexion as the textual authority of Augustine or Origen.

The way in which the matter came to my notice was as follows: I had been reading a volume of unpublished writings of the great Syriac father Bar Ṣalibi, in which he discourses against the Mohammedans, the Jews, the Nestorians, etc.; we may call it briefly a book against "Jews, Turks and Heretics."

In reading the first of the tracts which was written against the Moslems, I was much struck by the use which the controversialist made of arguments of an exactly similar character to those which I knew to have been employed by the early Christian

Fathers against the Jews, and I began to suspect that he had, either by tradition, or, which was more probable, in writing, a Syriac collection of early Christian *Testimonies against the Jews*. Certainly he must have been familiar with the primitive methods of Christian propagandism and debate.   And this belief was confirmed, and I think finally established, when I came recently to read the tract of Bar Ṣalibi against the Jews, which followed this one against the Moslems.   We shall show that in this tract Bar Ṣalibi definitely admits that he is working off a collection of Testimonies, and we shall see what he says on the subject of Judas.

The reader who is interested in the parallel between the Christian Father confuting the Jew, and the Christian Bishop disputing with the Moslem, will find an exact parallel in Mrs Gibson's Arabic tract from Mount Sinai, which she calls *A Tract on the Triune Nature of God*[1], but which I maintain should be simply headed *Against the Moslems*.   In reviewing this book in the *American Journal of Theology*[2], it was easy to establish the statement that "behind the writer we see the line of earlier scribes whose themes are inscribed *Contra Judaeos*: he has borrowed from them, used their methods, and incorporated their quotations," and at the close of the review it is claimed as demonstrated that there is an affinity of the tract with the earlier anti-Judaic literature and that the Eastern Church stood towards the Moslems in much the same position that they had occupied from the beginning toward the men of the Synagogue.   A similar state of mind to that of the writer of the anonymous tract is betrayed by Bar Ṣalibi. Let us now come to his actual arguments with the Jews, and see how he is in the habit of presenting his case.   I am now quoting from a MS. in my possession; the writer is establishing the doctrine of the Trinity and the Divine Nature of Jesus from the Scriptures; he presents his case in the following manner:

Jeremiah.   And I will raise up to David a branch of righteousness.

David.   Blessed is he that cometh in the name of the Lord.

Isaiah.   And he did not send an angel but the Lord Himself saved us.

Solomon, speaking as from the mouth of the Son, says: "Before the abysses I was brought forth."

Isaiah.   The Lord God hath sent me, and His Spirit.

Moses.   Thy right hand, O Lord, hath broken in pieces the enemy. (Here the arm and the right hand of the Father is the Son.)

---

[1] *Studia Sinaitica,* VII.

[2] *Am. Journ. Theol.* 1901, pp. 75–76, and previous chapter.

And so the writer goes on, coming at last to the conclusion that "all these things we have made clear from the *testimonies*."

Those who are familiar with the writings of Justin, Irenaeus, Tertullian, Cyprian, etc., will at once recognize familiar friends amongst the quotations. For example, the quotation from Moses (Ex. xv. 6), with its added explanation, corresponds to the section in Cyprian's *Testimonies* (Bk II. 4) which is headed "Quod Christus idem manus et brachium Dei," though the quotation itself does not appear in Cyprian. (Notice that the "arm" has not been mentioned in the text Bar Ṣalibi quotes.) In the same way, the editorial remark that Solomon speaks in the person of the Son, will be found in the *Testimonies against the Jews* ascribed to Gregory of Nyssa in the form: "Speaking in the person of Wisdom," *that is, of the Son* (he said), "When he was preparing the heaven I was by him." The passage from Is. lxiii. 9 is a well-known Christological argument, employed by Irenaeus (III. xxii. 1), Cyprian (*Testimonies*, II. 7) and elsewhere. And so we might accumulate a mass of references in confirmation of our statement that Bar Ṣalibi is here using not only the method of *Testimonies against the Jews*, but an actual collection. The minute agreements between himself and the early Christian Fathers and centoists can hardly be explained in any other way.

A little lower down he comes to Testimonies on the Passion and the Betrayal, and proceeds as follows:

Am. (v. 12). Concerning Judas who betrayed him, Amos prophesied, the oppressor of the righteous has taken a bribe.

Zech. (xii. 12), and Zechariah: If it be pleasing in your eyes, give me my price; and if not, you defraud me: and they weighed me thirty pieces of silver, and I took the thirty pieces of silver and cast them into the treasury.

And Jeremiah said: And they gave me the thirty pieces of silver, the price of the valued one, whom they valued from the sons of Israel, and I gave them for the potter's field.

Isa. (iii. 10). And Isaiah said: Woe to the wicked: because the evil of the work of their hands shall be recompensed.

Ps. lxviii. 27 and David: Command evil upon him, etc. And Ps. cix. 8: And his dwellings and his ministry let another take.

Prov. (vi. 12, 13). And Solomon says: A foolish person: a wicked man walks in slander: and he makes signs with his eyes and strikes with his fist.

Deut. (xxvii. 25). And Moses says: Cursed is everyone that taketh a bribe to kill the soul of the righteous.

Here then we have Bar Ṣalibi's Testimonies concerning Judas, and I think there will be little difficulty in conceding that they represent an older student than Bar Salibi himself. The text of the *Testimonies* follows closely the text of the Peshito, the sentence quoted from Jeremiah being a transcript from the Gospel of Matthew in that version. It does not, however, follow that it was originally taken from Matthew, for in the Syriac version the name of the prophet is wanting. The structure of Bar Ṣalibi's work implies, as we have shown above, a collection of written Testimonies in Greek, and it is quite natural that Bar Ṣalibi, or his sources, should give the well-known Syriac equivalents for them. One of the most interesting confirmations of the antiquity of the *Book of Testimonies* in Syriac will arise from the fact that it was clearly known to the author of the *Doctrine of Addai*. He represents Addai as using the method of *Testimonies* for the conversion of the people of Edessa, and actually gives the quotation from Is. xlviii. 16, which we have alluded to above, in the following form:

Also the prophets of old spake thus: that "the Lord our God and His Spirit hath sent us." And if I speak anything which is not written in the prophets, the Jews who are standing among you and hear me will not receive it[1].

Here then we come upon the suggestion that there existed a primitive collection of *Testimonies*, which has been used in its Greek form by St Matthew, and in its Syriac form by Bar Salibi. And the error of St Matthew, if it be an error, is due to his use of the *Book of Testimonies*. At this point the result of the investigation is somewhat different from what I expected. I was on the look out for evidence to show that the ascription to Jeremiah was one of those cases of which the *Testimonies* furnish frequent instances where a title has been misplaced; that is to say, I thought the title Zechariah had slipped, or had been displaced by the title of a neighbouring Testimony from Jeremiah. That would be a very easy solution to the whole difficulty; but it appears to be too simple; for (1) the evidence has increased for writing Jeremiah, not only in Matthew, where it certainly belongs, but in the previous document; (2) the title of Zechariah has not been displaced, for both Zechariah and Jeremiah are there; (3) there appears to be no other Jeremiah passage in the neighbourhood from which the title can have come. Moreover, when we examine the text of the prophecy-loving Matthew, on the hypothesis that

---

[1] Cf. Acts xxvi. 22, 23, where the heading of a section of Testimonies is in the text.

he is using a collection of *Testimonies*, we find that in Matt. xxvii. 16 (οἱ δὲ ἔστησαν αὐτῷ τριάκοντα ἀργύρια) there is a distinct trace of Zechariah xi. 12, as in Bar Salibi's extract, without the τὸν μισθόν μου. So that it really seems as if Matthew had used, from his little text-book, first a sentence from Zechariah, and second, one from Jeremiah (or, if you prefer it) Pseudo-Jeremiah.

My suggestion, then, is that the printed Greek text of Matthew is correct, but that it depends upon a lost collection of *Testimonies*; and it is no longer as obvious as it has sometimes been assumed to be, that the reference to Jeremiah ought to be explained away by the interpreter, where the textual critic has insisted on retaining it.

The inquiry must, clearly, be taken further; we have, however, gained a point, and, as Dr Robinson would say, "we must try and learn the lesson."

One part of the lesson would appear to be that the *Book of Testimonies* is older than much of the New Testament literature; whether we ought also to say that the Gospel of Matthew is later than has been commonly supposed is an interesting question which also requires more time and further deliberation.

CHAPTER VII

IRENAEUS AND THE BOOK OF TESTIMONIES

It will be seen from our introductory chapter that Irenaeus is one of the authorities for the existence of a book of quotations from the Old Testament, to be used by primitive Christians in their inevitable controversies with their brethren of the Jewish faith. We were able at once to infer, from a comparison of the way that Irenaeus introduces some verses from Isaiah xxxv. with the way in which the same verses are presented by Justin Martyr, that both Irenaeus and Justin took their quotations of Isaiah, not directly from the prophet, but from some text-book which they were both in the habit of employing. It will be interesting and illuminating to take the matter of the relation of Irenaeus and his supposed text-book of prophecies a little further, and to do this, we will not begin with the five books of Irenaeus *Against Heresies*, but with the newly-found treatise of Irenaeus *On the Apostolic Preaching*. Let us see what can be deduced from this early book of doctrine for the purposes of our inquiry. Does the new treatise confirm the suppositions which we had already been led to make by the consideration of certain passages in the great work against Heresies? In order to answer this question, we reprint an article which we wrote on the subject of the *Apostolic Preaching* in the *Expositor* for March 1907.

IRENAEUS ON THE APOSTOLICAL PREACHING.

We have now before us the text of the newly-found treatise of Irenaeus *On the Apostolical Preaching*, which forms the first part of the thirty-first volume of Harnack's *Texte und Untersuchungen*. More exactly we should have put, instead of Harnack, the joint names of Harnack and Schmidt, and that collocation would have at once reminded us that another of the great patristic lights has gone out, and that the long-continued co-operation of von Gebhardt and Harnack has been ended in the way in which the best-established of partnerships must be broken up at the last. The record of von Gebhardt's literary work remains, and it will not be easy, even for a well-trained and capable scholar, to succeed him.

But here is Irenaeus, fresh from the press, and full of interest and surprises. To begin with, a discovery of second-century literature can never be anything but interesting, in view of the fact that it was in this century that the organization and doctrine of the Church were really established; and the interest is unusual in the case of a writer like Irenaeus, who claims to be in touch with the Apostolical tradition through Papias and Polycarp and the elders who had known the Apostle John. As is well known, we have the already extant works of Irenaeus only through translation or by quotation; his great work, the five books against Heresies, is only known from the Latin translation, with the supplement of a few Greek, Syriac, and Armenian quotations; the original Greek is supposed by Zahn to have been extant in the sixteenth century; and, although doubt has been cast on his argument, we are not without hope that a complete copy of the original work may yet be lurking somewhere. But beside the five books against Heresies, there are traces of a number of other writings which have either wholly, or in great part, perished. Fragments are extant of certain letters to Florinus, in which Irenaeus warns him against the erroneous nature of the beliefs which he was embracing, and holds Polycarp up to him *in terrorem*. He wrote also certain other tracts relating to controversial matters of the time, such as the date of the Easter festival; and we learn from Eusebius that he dedicated a treatise to one Marcianus *On the Apostolical Preaching*, and it is this treatise which has suddenly come to light from as unexpected a quarter as could have been conceived, the library of the Armenian Church at Erivan, in Russian Armenia, where it was unearthed in 1904 by one of the most able of the younger Armenian ecclesiastics, Karabet ter-Mekerttschian. He has now edited the text in collaboration with his friend, ter-Minassiantz, accompanied by a German translation of such fidelity and excellence that it needed very little emendation at the hand of Harnack and his editorial office. I was in Erivan in 1903, and had the pleasure of visiting these learned Armenians at the great convent of Etschmiadzin; little suspecting, as we examined the treasures of their great library, that a patristic document of the first magnitude was lying only a few miles away and waiting to be discovered. We may at least take heart in two directions: first, in the belief that it is still reasonable to expect the recovery of the lost documents of the early Church; and second, that the Armenian people have given us one more proof that they are not the dying race which they are, in many quarters, assumed to be; but that in the region of religion, as well as in that of science, they are, as I have often maintained publicly, the brain of Asia.

The first reading of the new book will, I think, cause something of a sense of disappointment; it appears to be wanting in originality. This is partly due to the fact that it is a catechetical treatise, following the conventional lines of the teaching of the Church of the second century, and using the same arguments and proof-texts as are found elsewhere in that period and the time immediately subsequent. The Gospels are *not* the foundation of the argument, the whole weight of which is thrown upon the Old Testament, that is to say, upon the prophecies, together with the allegorical and mystical explanation of the histories. At first sight this is both surprising and disappointing, for Irenaeus is instructing his friend Marcianus in the very foundations of the Faith, and he hardly uses the Gospel at all; everything is prophecy and gnosis, just as it is with Justin Martyr; and the Gospels, which Irenaeus speaks of elsewhere, in a well-known passage, as comparable to the four pillars of the world and the four winds of heaven, take relatively less place than they do in Justin Martyr. The fault is in the method of teaching, which Irenaeus has clearly inherited. His real gospel is the *Book of Testimonies*, concerning the use of which we have written in our introductory Chapter. We will return to this point presently. But the fault, as it seems to us, is the more patent when we remember that the book before us is probably one of the last things that Irenaeus ever wrote. He refers to his great work on Heresies, which can hardly have been completed much before 190 A.D., so that the new tract must belong to the last decade of the second century. One would have supposed that, by this date, the Gospels would have taken their right place in the education of a catechumen, and that the Person of Christ would have been presented historically, and not by the method of obscure and often impossible reflections from the Prophets or the Psalms.

So far is Irenaeus from using the historical foundations of Christianity, that he does not even know how old Christ was when He died, nor what emperor He died under. There is a well-known passage in the *Adv. Haereses*, II. 22, which has caused grave searchings of heart, because it implied a belief (based, perhaps, in the first instance, on a misunderstood passage of St John's Gospel) that our Lord must have been nearly fifty years of age, in opposition to the common belief that He was little more than thirty years when He finished His public ministry. And here, in the Apostolical Preaching, we are quietly informed that He suffered under Pontius Pilate (so far we are following the Apostolical Symbol), but that Pontius Pilate was the procurator *under the emperor Claudius*. It will be very difficult, in view of the known procuratorship of Pontius Pilate under Tiberius, and his subsequent recall, to trust Irenaeus in any matter that requires the exercise of the historical sense; for if chronology is one of the eyes of history, he has deliberately put that eye out. We must not look to the new tract (nor to the old author) for historical details. Its value, and his, lie in another direction.

The argument of the book is as follows. One attains truth through purity of soul and body: through right thinking and right acting, through right belief and right love. Right belief consists in knowing the things that really are (τὰ ὄντα): it is a doctrine of God the Father, God the Son, and God the Holy Ghost. The Holy Ghost brings us to the knowledge of the Son, the Son to the knowledge of the Father. The world was created by the Word of God, and was made for a habitation of men, to whom is given lordship over the angels. Irenaeus then proceeds to summarize the whole of the history of the world, from the Creation, Fall, Flood, Call of Abraham, and so on, down to the building of the Temple, and the rise of the Prophets. (In writing the history of the flood, he borrows freely from the Book of Enoch.) The Prophets declare the Incarnation of Christ and the redemption of men. The Virgin Birth is proved by the prophecies and by an Old Testament gnosis which makes Mary the second Eve. A few lines are given to the preaching of John the Baptist and to the works and sufferings of Christ recorded in the Gospels. After which the writer returns to the Old Testament and the theology supposed to be latent in it, with regard to the Deity and Pre-existence of Christ. A casual reference is made to John the disciple of the Lord and the opening sentence of his Gospel. The order and method of the *Book of Testimonies* are closely followed, and after establishing all the main points of the Gospel account from the Old Testament, he concludes that "*these testimonies* show His Davidic descent, according to the flesh, and His birth in the city of David"; we are not to look for His birth among the heathen *or anywhere else but in Bethlehem.* His works and sufferings were also foretold. It is surprising that the teaching of Christ is almost entirely absent; His sayings are not quoted, and, more disappointing still, there are no apocryphal sayings or new words of Jesus. The writer concludes with a little warning against the heresies of the time, which are classified as heresies concerning the Father, the Son, and the Holy Spirit. We must not divide the Father from the Creator, we must not depreciate or deny the Incarnation, and we must not undervalue the gifts of the Holy Spirit, especially the prophetic gift, for it is through these gifts that life becomes fruitful.

Such being the structure of the book, we repeat that the first reading is somewhat disappointing, even when we agree with Harnack that there are directions in which it makes a great impression upon us: as, for example, in the complete absence of hierarchical and ceremonial elements, and in the relatively small position given to the Sacraments. Church authority and tradition are not appealed to; they are latent, but not directly affirmed. The sum of the doctrine of Irenaeus is that a life of faith in God is a life of love to man. We wish he had divided his subject a little more evenly, and given more place to the human relations of the Christian man. In this respect he does not come near to the ethical elevation of Aristides, for example. But now, having done with preliminary disappointments, let us turn to the text and see what light we can throw on some of the passages.

In the first place, we have the important evidence of a quotation from Polycarp's Epistle to the Philippians. Up to the present we had no early quotation from Polycarp, and the external evidence for his Epistle was limited (as far as the first two centuries after its composition are concerned) to a statement of Irenaeus (*Haer.* III. 3, 4), in which he declares that—

There is a very adequate letter of Polycarp written to the Philippians, from which those who desire it, and who care for their own salvation, can learn both the character of his faith and the message of the truth.

Now let us turn to the *Apostolical Preaching*, c. 95:

> Through faith in the Son of God, we learn to love God with all our heart and our neighbour as ourselves. But *love to God is far from all sins*, and love to the neighbour causes no evil to the neighbour.

Compare with this the following from Polycarp, *ad Phil.* 3:

> Faith is the mother of us all, followed by hope, in front of whom goes love to God and to Christ and to the neighbour. For if one be within these, he has fulfilled the law of righteousness; *for he that hath love is far from all sin.*

The coincidence in words is reinforced by the coincidence of the whole argument, and there cannot be any doubt that Irenaeus is using Polycarp, with whose writings he shows himself in another passage to be acquainted. It is curious that Harnack does not seem to have noticed the quotation, any more than the Armenian editors; but it is of some importance critically.

Another interesting case of an unidentified quotation will be found in c. 77. Here we are told, amongst the prophecies of the Passion, to reckon the following:

> It is said in the book of the Twelve Prophets: they chained him and brought him there to the king as a present. For Pontius Pilate was the procurator of Judaea, and was at that time at enmity with Herod, the king of the Jews. But after, when Christ was brought to him in chains, Pilate sent Him to Herod, leaving him to examine Him, in order to know exactly what he would do with Him, using Christ as an excuse for reconciliation with the king.

Here the editors are at fault, and Harnack adds that to the best of his knowledge there is no such passage in the Minor Prophets, and that it is significant that Irenaeus, in this instance, does not give the name of the prophet whom he is quoting.

The passage is Hosea x. 6, which the LXX presents in the following form:

καὶ αὐτὸν εἰς Ἀσσυρίους δήσαντες, ἀπήνεγκαν ξένια τῷ βασιλεῖ Ἰαρείμ.

It is not easy to see how this Greek was made out of the Hebrew, as we know it; and it is well known that the passages relating to King Jarib are to this day a *crux interpretum*. But that the passage was taken as a prophetic Testimony to Christ and His trial, is certain. Suppose we turn to Justin, *Dialogue with Trypho*, c. 103; here we find as follows:

Ἡρώδου δὲ, τὸν Ἀρχέλαον διαδεξαμένου, λαβόντος τὴν ἐξουσίαν τὴν ἀπονεμηθεῖσαν αὐτῷ, ᾧ καὶ Πιλάτος χαριζόμενος δεδεμένον τὸν Ἰησοῦν ἔπεμψε, καὶ τοῦτο γενησόμενον προειδὼς ὁ θεὸς εἰρήκει οὕτως· καίγε αὐτὸν εἰς Ἀσσυρίους ἀπήνεγκαν ξένια τῷ βασιλεῖ.

Here Justin makes the same connexion as Irenaeus between the passage in Hosea and the account of what passed between Pilate and Herod.

The same connexion is made in Tertullian against Marcion (IV. 42):

Nam et Herodi velut munus a Pilato missus, Osee vocibus fidem reddidit: de Christo enim prophetaverat: et vinctum eum ducent xeniam regi.

Tertullian, as is well known, used the prophetic Testimonies in slaying Marcion; and I think it is now clear that both he and Justin are using a formal collection of such Testimonies; for the connexion between Hosea and the Gospel is by no means obvious, even to a person whose mind was set on finding Christ in the Old Testament. In any case, there can be no doubt where Irenaeus' quotation comes from. We shall find the same connexion made in Cyril of Jerusalem (*Cat.* XIII. 14) as follows: δεθεὶς ἦλθεν ἀπὸ τοῦ Καϊάφα πρὸς Πιλάτον· ἄρα καὶ τοῦτο γέγραπται· καὶ δήσαντες αὐτὸν ἀπήνεγκαν ξένια τῷ βασιλεῖ Ἰαρείμ. And also in Ruffinus on the Symbol.

And this brings us to the interesting question of the relation of the composition, and of the catechetical teaching which underlies it, to the collection of prophetic passages which I have shown to be current in the early Church, whose original title seems to have been *Testimonies against the Jews*. Does the new treatise involve Irenaeus in the use of that early book in the way that I have suggested in the introductory chapter? For example, we are to ask whether it quotes the same proof-texts as the *Book of Testimonies*, whether it quotes them with similar sequences, with the same misunderstandings, like combinations, similar displacements of the names of authors quoted, and so on.

Perhaps it will be sufficient if I present a few striking cases of coincidence in the matter quoted from the Old Testament and in the manner in which it is quoted.

It will be remembered that I drew attention to the way in which Bar Salibi, in his *Testimonies against the Jews*, quotes as follows:

David said: Before the day-star I begat thee. And before the sun is his name and before the moon. Now explain to us, when was Israel born before the day-star, etc.

The combination of passages from the 110th Psalm and the 71st Psalm was noted, and it was shown that the same two passages were combined in Justin, *Dialogue*, c. 76, and in the collection of prophetic extracts ascribed to Gregory of Nyssa.

Now turn to the new treatise, c. 43, and you will find Irenaeus establishing the pre-existence of Christ from the first verse of the book of Genesis, after which he goes on:

> And Jeremiah the prophet also testifies this as follows: Before the morning-star have I begotten thee, and before the sun is his name.

Here the very same sequence occurs, in exact agreement with Bar Salibi; and we have, over and above that coincidence, an error of ascription such as frequently occurs in these collections, by which Jeremiah is made responsible for the Psalms! Probably, though I have not been able to verify this, a proof-text from Jeremiah lay adjacent[1]. A similar case exists in our Gospel of Matthew with reference to the potter's field, and the parallel is particularly interesting because Irenaeus quotes it in the newly-found treatise, and evidently *not* from the Gospel. His language is as follows:

> c. 81: And again Jeremiah the prophet said: "And they took the thirty pieces of silver, the price of the one that was sold, whom they of the children of Israel had bought, and gave them for the potter's field, as the Lord commanded me." For Judas, who was of Christ's disciples, etc.

A comparison of the other passages which are similarly treated will show that Irenaeus means to quote the prophet, and does not mean to quote the Gospel. From which again we infer that the famous reading stood in a book of *Testimonies*.

Another famous passage to which I referred was the prophecy of Jacob concerning Judah ("the sceptre shall not fail from Judah," etc.), which I showed to have been current in the *Book of Testimonies* as a prophecy of Moses (see Iren., *adv. Haer.* IV. 10, and Justin, I. *Ap.* 32). In c. 57 of the new treatise we get the same matter brought forward, with the preface, "And Moses says in Genesis," the change in the manner of introducing the passage being made so as to avoid the error of the ascription of the prophecy to Moses. Then, after explaining the meaning of the blessing of Judah, and how he washes his garments in wine, which is a symbol of eternal joy, he goes on, "And on this account he is also the hope of the heathen, *who hope in him*." This addition becomes

---

[1] The missing proof-text will be found later on.

clearer if we assume that somewhere in the neighbourhood of the words he was quoting (αὐτὸς προσδοκία ἐθνῶν) there stood the words:

> καὶ ἐπὶ τὸν βραχίονα αὐτοῦ ἔθνη ἐλπιοῦσιν·

for when we refer to the parallel section in Justin Martyr (ι. *Ap.* 32) we find as follows:

> καὶ 'Ησαίας δέ, ἄλλος προφήτης, τὰ αὐτὰ δι' ἄλλων ῥήσεων προφητεύων, οὕτως εἶπεν, 'Ανατελεῖ ἄστρον ἐξ 'Ιακὼβ καὶ ἄνθος ἀναβήσεται ἀπὸ τῆς ῥίζης 'Ιεσσαί· καὶ ἐπὶ τὸν βραχίονα αὐτοῦ ἔθνη ἐλπιοῦσιν

(Num. xxiv. 17; Isa. xi. 1; xi. 10),

where the sequence of thought is again preserved for us which occurs in the argument in Irenaeus. And if we read on in Irenaeus, we shall find the words actually extant which he has proleptically treated at the end of c. 57. The order of the passages in the original book can be clearly made out. And the same thing can be shown elsewhere in the new treatise, but for brevity I forbear further reference to this matter.

Here is one other curious and interesting passage in which the treatment of prophecies by Irenaeus is closely parallel to that which we find in Justin, but apparently without any direct dependence of the former upon the latter.

In c. 70, in dealing with Christ's sufferings, Irenaeus quotes from Isaiah liii. 8 ("Who shall declare His generation?"). He then goes on (c. 71) to quote Lamentations iv. 20 under the name of Jeremiah; and then (c. 72) to point out from the same prophet (it should have been Isaiah) "how the righteous perish and no man layeth it to heart; and pious men are taken away" (Isa. lvii. 1); and proceeds to prove from it (i) the death of Christ, (ii) the sufferings of those who are His followers; and neither of these points would have been made by a rational exegete; and he concludes thus:

> Who, says the prophet, is perfectly righteous except the Son of God, who leads on those who believe in him to perfect righteousness, *who are persecuted and killed like himself?*

Here the parallel in Justin Martyr, ι. *Ap.* 48, is very striking:

> And as to the way he pointed out in advance by the prophetic spirit, that he should be done to death *along with those who hope in him,* listen to the things that were spoken by Isaiah, etc.[1]

---

[1] Πῶς τε προμεμήνυται ὑπὸ τοῦ προφητικοῦ πνεύματος ἀναιρεθησόμενος ἅμα τοῖς ἐπ' αὐτὸν ἐλπίζουσιν, ἀκούσατε τῶν λεχθέντων διὰ 'Ησαίου.

I do not think that the coincidence, which we here observe in
the treatment of the passage in Isaiah at the hands of Irenaeus
and Justin, is due to the fact that Irenaeus has been reading
Justin; it is more natural to suppose that the treatment of the
passage is conventional and is invited by a headline in the *Testimony Book*. But enough has probably been said on this point.
The inference which we draw is something more than our previous
conclusions: we not only confirm our argument as to the existence
of written collections of prophecies used for controversial purposes
against the Jews, but since the treatise we have before us is almost
the equivalent of a Church Catechism, we see that the *Book of
Testimonies* became a regular book of Church teaching, and that
it passed out of controversial use with Jews into doctrinal use for
the instruction of Greeks, and that, being so used, it is, as we
have said above, the equivalent of a Gospel for the instruction of
the catechumens; a little later and it will be displaced by the
Gospels themselves, and will rapidly disappear.

Now, in conclusion, we may point out that the anti-Judaic
character of the early Apostolical Preaching which Irenaeus is
commending to Marcianus is reflected in the ethics of the book,
which, although meagre in quantity, are lofty in tone and anti-
Judaic in temper. The writer has no further use for the Mosaic
Law! Why should we tell a man not to kill, who does not even
hate? or not to covet his neighbour's goods when he loves his
neighbour as himself? or why tell him to keep an idle day of rest
every week, when he keeps every day a Sabbath rest in himself?
Is not the true temple the human body, where God is constantly
served in righteousness? As for sacrifices, read what Isaiah says
about the sacrifice of an ox being the equivalent of the offering
of a dog.

Could anything be more characteristically anti-Judaic, or more
definitely Christian? And this is the teaching which professes to
present the Apostolical tradition; it has none of the natural
machinery of religion, and very little supernatural machinery;
the terrors of the world to come are as little in evidence as the
offerings of bulls and goats. The proportion of the doctrines
presented is certainly significant. We should have expected more
in this direction and less in that, more in the direction of ritual
and less in the direction of ethics unqualified by eschatology.
But it would clearly be going too far to assume an argument

from silence, and say that Irenaeus had no ritual conceptions, and taught no eschatology. For we have the five books against Heresies to reckon with, as well as a number of preserved fragments from lost books[1].

It seems clear, however, that the tradition which he presents made much of the interior change and of the spiritual enlightenment. And it is in reference to this spiritual vision and experience that we come nearest to the actual teaching of the New Testament. In c. 93 Irenaeus quotes the famous passage from Hosea (ii. 25), where the Not-Beloved becomes Beloved, and the Not-People the children of the living God. For, says he, this is what John the Baptist meant when he said, "God can raise up children to Abraham from the stones." *For after our hearts have been torn away from their stony service and made free, then we behold God by faith and become the children of Abraham, those, namely, who are justified by faith.*

So far I had written on the subject of the Use of Testimonies in the *Apostolical Preaching* of Irenaeus in 1907. On reading the treatise over again, it is clear that the matter has not been overstated of the dependence of Irenaeus on a *Testimony Book*: many more illustrations might have been given. The conclusions to which we came were arrived at also by Minucci in the *Rivista di Storia Critica della Sc. Teol.* (III. 134).

We may, with advantage, spend a little more time on the Testimonies of the *Apostolical Preaching*, before we go on to collect further data from other writers.

For example in c. 43 we are told that

The Son of God not only existed before his appearance in the world, but even before the existence of the world, as Moses was the first to prophesy: he says in Hebrew:

Bareşiṭ bara elowim başam benuam samanṭares:

which in our language is translated:

"Son at the beginning—God founded then the Heaven and the earth."

[1] It should be noticed that the parallels between the *adv. Haer.* and the *Apostolic Preaching* are constant and often very illuminating. For instance, in c. 14 Irenaeus explains the innocence of Adam and Eve in the garden by the fact that they were created as boy and girl: and, as Harnack notes, this was already implied in *adv. Haer.* III. 22. 3 (Erant enim utrique nudi in Paradiso et non confundebantur, quoniam paulo ante facti, non intellectum habebant filiorum generationis: oportebat enim illos primos adolescere, dehinc sic multiplicari). See also the curious argument for the Virgin Birth in c. 36, based on the promise to David, "Of the fruit of thy body, etc." and the same argument in *adv. Haer.* III. 21. 5.

And this also the prophet Jeremiah testifies as follows: *Before the morning-star I begat thee, and before the sun is his name.* That means before the making of the world, for the stars came into being along with the world. And again he says: *Blessed is he, who was there before the coming of man into being.* Since the Son had his beginning as far as God is concerned (κατὰ τὸν Θεόν) before the foundation of the world, but as far as we are concerned (καθ' ἡμᾶς) at the time of his actual appearance. Before this time he did not exist for us, that is, who did not know him. And that is why his disciple John said: (then follows the opening of the Fourth Gospel).

We need not spend time over the restoration of the transliterated Hebrew of Gen. i. 1. The beginning is clear enough, down to *elohim*: the end of the verse should be *eth-haššamayim w'eth haareṣ,* so it looks as if some fresh word or words had been inserted in the middle. The natural suggestion is that *bara* has been taken to mean *the Son,* and another verb intruded. It is well known that the early exegetes did try to find the Son in the first words of Genesis.

We pass on to notice that a composite quotation from the Psalms, which we have previously discussed, is here ascribed to Jeremiah. As Irenaeus certainly knew better than to credit Jeremiah with well-worn extracts from the Psalms, we conclude that the error is again in the *Testimony Book,* probably from a marginal confusion of references. There should have been, one suspects, a Jeremiah quotation in the neighbourhood.

Then we come to the most curious feature of all, an anonymous reference, or perhaps a second reference to Jeremiah.

And again he says: *Blessed is he who was there before the coming of man into being.*

Harnack remarks that he has in vain sought for the origin of this apocryphal saying. It is certainly very perplexing; we note, however, that it turns up elsewhere.

We shall have occasion to show in a subsequent chapter that Lactantius in the fourth book of his *Divine Institutes* is working steadily at the *Testimony Book*; here is the opening of the eighth chapter.

De ortu Jesu in Spiritu et in carne : de spiritibus et testimoniis prophetarum. In primis enim testificamur, illum bis esse natum: primum in spiritu, postea in carne. Unde apud Hieremiam ita dicitur: *Priusquam te formarem in utero, novi te.* Et item apud ipsum: *Beatus qui erat, antequam nasceretur*; quod nulli alii contigit praeter Christum.

Here then we find a Latin text which corresponds to what we
find in the Armenian of Irenaeus, with slight variation. This
time we are told expressly to refer the citation to Jeremiah, and
the language of Irenaeus will bear this construction if a quotation
from Jeremiah precedes. "Again he says" means in this case,
"Jeremiah says again."

We notice further the coincidence between Irenaeus and
Lactantius, in the attempt to prove that the Son had two births,
one in the spirit (κατὰ θεόν) and the other in the flesh (κατὰ σάρκα).
It is not easy to make the language bear an orthodox interpretation. It is, however, clear that they are both working at Testimonies: the false reference of Irenaeus to Jeremiah is due to his
having eliminated the proof-text "Before I formed thee in the
womb I knew thee." That was a little too much of an intellectual
strain, even for Irenaeus. With Lactantius, however, the quotation held its ground, and the reference to Jeremiah was in order.

What, now, is the origin of the sentence:

> Beatus qui erat, antequam nasceretur:
> Blessed is he who was there before becoming man?

I think the whole of the confusion is due to a misinterpretation of
Ps. lxxi. 17

> ἔστω τὸ ὄνομα αὐτοῦ εὐλογημένον εἰς τοὺς αἰῶνας· πρὸ τοῦ ἡλίου διαμενεῖ
> τὸ ὄνομα αὐτοῦ.

Part of the verse has already been quoted by Irenaeus,

> Before the Sun is his name.

The other part of the verse is an attempt to say

> His name was blessed before the Sun.

All the material for the confusion is at hand in the famous verse
from the Psalm. The original form was perhaps: He was blessed
before the sun (antequam nasceretur sol). If we wanted further
proof that Lactantius was at this very point transcribing from his
Testimony Book, the following observation may suffice.

Lactantius' reference goes on in the following strain:

> *Beatus qui erat, antequam nasceretur;* quod nulli alii contigit, praeter
> Christum. Qui cum esset a principio Filius Dei, regeneratus est denuo secun-
> dum carnem.

Now turn to Cyprian, *Test.* II. 8. The reading of the section
is as follows:

> Quod cum a principio Filius Dei fuisset, generari denuo haberet secundum
> carnem.

We see that Lactantius has actually incorporated the heading of the chapter. There can, therefore, be no doubt that he is working at his *Testimony Book*. We learn something more. Cyprian also has the doctrine of the two births of Christ; his headline shows that, though he has only a single Old Testament reference on the subject. Apparently he has dropped the further proof-texts. Irenaeus also is drawing on the same headline, as his reference to the dual birth of Christ will show.

All three writers, Irenaeus, Cyprian, Lactantius, are working on the same theme, with a common body of proof-texts.

It is somewhat disconcerting to find that the primitive document which we have tracked down was so defective in common sense as to find a proof of the pre-existence of the Son in the words which describe the fore-ordination of Jeremiah, and that, of the writers whom we have been comparing, the most eloquent and most highly educated of the three should persist in the supposed proof, and not suspect its irrationality.

A knowledge of the existing *Testimony Books* would have been of great service to the editors and exponents of Irenaeus' newly-found treatise. For example, in c. 80 the editors have left a sentence untranslated. They say in a foot-note that the "passage is apparently corrupt. It might mean 'and my body by nails,' or with a slight change, 'Nail on my body.'"

If we look at Cyprian, *Test*. II. 20, we shall find the missing sentence referred to the 118th (119th) Psalm:

> Confige clavis (de metu tuo) carnes meas:

or in Greek

> καθήλωσον τὰς σάρκας μου (Psalm cxix. 120).

There is no doubt that nearly the whole of the treatise of Irenaeus on the *Apostolical Preaching* is a commentary on a collection of Testimonies.

One point more may be noted in passing. We have shown in the previous chapter the real meaning of the perplexing reference to Jeremy the prophet in the Gospel of Matthew (xxvii. 10) and have claimed the sentences about the purchase of the potter's field for prophetical Testimonies. Meanwhile we may register the observation, that we have the same kind of confusion in the new Irenaeus, without any reference to Matthew, as far as the quotation is concerned.

In the 81st chapter we read as follows: "And again the prophet Jeremiah said: 'and they took the thirty pieces of silver, the price of him that was sold, whom they of the children of Israel had bought, and they gave them for the potter's field, as the Lord had commanded me.'" Here the editors properly assign the references, Jer. xxxii. 6 ff., Zech. xi. 12 ff., and say cf. Matt. xxvii. 10.

CHAPTER VIII

LACTANTIUS AND THE *BOOK OF TESTIMONIES*

When the early Christian Father Lactantius addressed to Constantine the Great his work on Christian Apologetics, which he calls by the name of *Divine Institutes,* he incorporated as the fourth book of the series a treatise on the *True Wisdom and Religion*; and the editors of Lactantius (Buneman, Isaeus, Dufresnoy, etc.) when they came upon this treatise soon found out that the arguments and the Biblical quotations in the treatise were often in agreement with Cyprian, and in particular with those parts of Cyprian's writings which comprise the three books of *Testimonies against the Jews.* It was something more than the use of an Old Latin Bible Text of a Cyprianic type; often the quotations were in coincidence; but the first editors were more concerned to give a correct text of Lactantius, and to use Cyprianic parallels for that end, than they were to ask whether the dependence of one author upon the other was real, and to find out the meaning of the dependence if it existed. So they simply give us an occasional cross reference to Cyprian.

The connexion between Lactantius and Cyprian should have been affirmed positively and then explained. A glance at Isaeus' notes on the fourth book of the *Institutes,* for example, will show the constant concurrence of the two writers. They are very seldom apart from one another in their quotations. Lactantius himself praises Cyprian and his writings in lib. v. c. 1, where he discusses him along with Minucius Felix and Tertullian.

Unus igitur praecipuus et clarus extitit Cyprianus, quoniam et magnam sibi gloriam ex artis oratoriae professione quaesierat, et admodum multa conscripsit in suo genere miranda.

There is no reason to doubt the acquaintance of Lactantius with the writings of Cyprian, and his admiration for the same.

Seeing that the fourth book of the *Divine Institutes* deals with the question of the true religion and its opposites from the stand-point of prophecy, and bases its demonstrations on the *Testimonies of the Prophets,* we are obliged to recognize that this is precisely the method of Cyprian, and to examine how far the coincidence in the method of demonstration really goes, and to what extent the same matter is extant in the actual quotations from which the two writers proceed. In this way we shall find out whether Lactantius is transcribing from Cyprian's own collection, or whether he is working like Cyprian upon the older base, which, for the latter writer underlies his first two books of *Testimonia.* If Lactantius is transcribing Cyprian, then we have an almost contemporary witness for the Cyprianic text, of the first importance for the determination of that text. If, however it should turn out that Lactantius is working from an earlier stratum of pro-phetic deposit, then the comparison of his text with that of Cyprian will help us to determine a more ancient form, from which they are both derived. So we must set the texts of the fourth book of the *Divine Institutes,* and the first two books of the *Testimonies against the Jews,* over against one another, and draw what conclusions we may from their agreement and divergence.

In one direction there will be divergence. Lactantius does not limit his prophetic writers to the Old Testament canon: though he does not, except in very rare instances, like Cyprian, add the N.T. passages that correspond to what he quotes from the Old Testament. He goes outside the canon altogether and brings in prophets and prophetesses from the pagan world, or assumed to be of pagan origin, Hermes Trismegistus and the Sibyl; these he quotes in Greek without translation. Both of the new witnessing elements are foreign to Cyprian. Yet it may be said as regards the Sibyls that Lactantius was not without a precedent in using them for the Christian evidences. The apologists of the second century not infrequently do the same, Theophilus for instance, in his address to Autolycus. It is quite possible that some of Lactantius' Sibylline extracts may have found their way into Christian handbooks before his day: at all events he has, in employing the Sibyls and Hermes, a larger crowd of witnesses than Cyprian.

Suppose we set aside the Sibylline and Hermetic matter, and examine what is left of the fourth book of the *Institutes,* which we can compare with Cyprian. The answer to the inquiry is that the same method is adopted in the two writers, and the quotations are almost identical. If Cyprian opens his first book with the proof that the Jews have grievously sinned against God, Lactantius has the same theme. If the Jews are by Cyprian taxed with ingratitude to their benefactors and leaders, to God and Moses and the prophets, the same is true of Lactantius, who tells us that "*God was offended* with them for the sin and crime of making the golden calf, and that He laid punishments upon *an impious and ungrateful people,* and put them *under the yoke of the law,* which He had given them by Moses."

This is anti-Judaic in the very same sense that the chapters of Cyprian's first book are anti-Judaic, where we are told

1. That the Jews have grievously sinned and offended God, in their forsaking the Lord and following idols.

....

8. That the former law which was given by Moses is now to cease.

If Cyprian calls his book by the name of *Testimonies,* Lactantius tells us (IV. 5) that he intends to say a few words about the prophets, whose *testimonies* he is going to employ, a method of demonstration which he had avoided in the previous books of the *Institutes.* Successive chapters are headed

7. *Testimonies* of the Sibyl and of Trismegistus to the Son of God.

8. *Testimonies* of the Prophets concerning the origin of Jesus, in spirit and in flesh.

So in c. 12 we have

Testimonies of the Prophets to the Virgin-birth, Life, Death and Resurrection of Jesus,

and in c. 13

Testimonies of the Prophets to the Divine and the Human Nature of Jesus.

If Cyprian devotes his fourth chapter of the first book to the thesis that (c. 4) "The Jews could not understand the Holy Scriptures, but they would become intelligible in the last time, after Christ had come":

Lactantius (IV. 15) tells us that the utterances of the prophets had been heard by the Jews for five hundred years, nor were they understood until Christ interpreted them by his word and his works. They could not have been understood until they had been fulfilled.

If Cyprian declares that, in consequence of the infidelity and

ingratitude of the Jews, there would have to be a new Covenant,
made with a new people, more faithful than the old,

> i. 11. Quod dispositio alia et testamentum novum dari haberet.
>
> ....
>
> 21. Quod gentes magis in Christum crediturae essent,

Lactantius, on his part, declares that the Jews have always
resisted sound teaching, *and gone after idolatrous worship*, and have
been reproved by the prophets *for their ingratitude*: they were
warned that God would *change His covenant*, and transfer the inheritance of immortal life to the Gentiles, and gather from amongst
aliens for Himself *a more faithful people* (c. 11).

It would be easy to amplify the illustrations of the coincidence
in method of the two writers; but it is hardly necessary, in view
of the conclusive proofs of the identity of the prophetic matter
presented by them.

If we take the fourth book of the *Divine Institutes*, and examine
the contents of chapters 6 to 21, we shall find that nearly all the
biblical extracts of Lactantius are in the first two books of Cyprian's
Testimonies, and that they frequently occur in the very same order,
with the very same introductory formulae. For example, the
section on the abolition of circumcision (quod circumcisio prima
carnalis evacuata sit etc.) has its proofs arranged as follows by
Cyprian (*Test.* I. 8)

> *Apud Hieremiam prophetam :*
>> Haec dicit Dominus, etc. (Jer. iv. 3 ff.)
>
> *Item Moyses dicit :*
>> In novissimis diebus, etc. (Deut. xxx. 6.)
>
> *Item apud Jesum Naue :*
>> Et dixit Dominus ad Jesum. (Jos. v. 2.)

In Lactantius we have

> *Esaias (sic !) ita prophetavit :*
>> Haec dicit Dominus, etc.
>
> *Item Moyses ipse :*
>> In novissimis diebus, etc.
>
> *Item Jesus Naue Successor eius :*
>> Et dixit Dominus ad Jesum.

Here the order is the same and the contents the same *quam
proxime*; the ascription of the first quotation to Isaiah is due to
the fact that Isaiah has been quoted a little while before: it is a
common type of error in citations of Testimonies.

Here is another example, where the coincidence is somewhat disturbed, but the underlying agreement can be detected: the prophecies relating to the crucifixion are arranged as follows:

Cyprian Test. II. 20.	Lactantius Instit. IV. 18.
Is. lxv. 2.	Esdras (?).
Jer. xi. 19.	Is. liii.
Deut. xxviii. 66.	Ps. xciii.
Ps. xxi. 17 ff.	Jer. xi. 19.
Ps. cxviii. 120.	Deut. xxviii. 66.
Ps. cxl. 2.	Num. xxiii. 19.
Zeph. i. 7.	Zach. xii. 10.
Zach. xii. 10.	Ps. xxi. 17 ff.
Ps. lxxxvii. 10.	1 Ki. ix. (?).
Num. xxiii. 19.	

Here five of the citations agree (and they are very curious citations): and it is easy to conjecture a primitive nucleus out of which the groups of prophetic Testimonies have been evolved. Speaking generally we may say that even if the order of sequence is varied from one writer to another, and if a lacuna can be detected in one writer relative to the other, we can generally find the missing passage somewhere else in Cyprian or Lactantius, and verify that their stock-in-trade of Testimonies is the same, and harmonize the incongruent sequences. Here, however, we touch on a most important question. There are a few passages in Lactantius that are conspicuously absent from Cyprian; can we say that these are inserted in the argument by Lactantius, or must we suggest that they have been dropped by Cyprian? For instance, in the last case which we were looking at Lactantius has (i) a passage which he refers to Esdras, (ii) a passage from the first book of Kings, which he expands in a unique and unexpected manner.

The first of these passages is as follows:

Apud Esdram ita scriptum erat: Et dixit Esdras ad populum: Hoc pascha Salvator noster est, et refugium nostrum. Cogitate, et ascendat in cor vestrum, quoniam habemus humiliare eum in signo, et post haec sperabimus in eum, ne deseratur hic locus in aeternum tempus, dicit Dominus Deus virtutum. Si non credideritis ei, neque exaudieritis annuntiationem eius, eritis derisio in gentibus.

Is this passage from an assumed Ezra book to be credited to Lactantius or did he find it in his sources? We turn to the *Dialogue* of Justin *with Trypho the Jew*, which of necessity is crammed with anti-Judaic proof-texts, and we find him complaining that the Jews have removed from the Old Testament many passages

which made against their religion; the first passage which he
quotes is the one to which we have been referring; it runs as
follows in Justin:

ἀπὸ μὲν οὖν τῶν ἐξηγήσεων, ὧν ἐξηγήσατο Ἔσδρας εἰς τὸν νόμον τὸν περὶ τοῦ
πάσχα, τὴν ἐξήγησιν ταύτην ἀφείλοντο.

καὶ εἶπεν Ἔσδρας τῷ λαῷ· τοῦτο τὸ πάσχα ὁ σωτὴρ ἡμῶν καὶ ἡ καταφυγὴ
ἡμῶν· καὶ ἐὰν διανοηθῆτε καὶ ἀναβῇ ὑμῶν ἐπὶ τὴν καρδίαν, ὅτι μέλλομεν αὐτὸν
ταπεινοῦν ἐν σημείῳ, καὶ μετὰ ταῦτα ἐλπίσωμεν ἐπ᾽ αὐτόν, οὐ μὴ ἐρημωθῇ ὁ τόπος
οὗτος εἰς τὸν ἅπαντα χρόνον, λέγει ὁ Θεὸς τῶν δυνάμεων. ἐὰν δὲ μὴ πιστεύσητε αὐτῷ,
μηδὲ εἰσακούσητε τοῦ κηρύγματος αὐτοῦ, ἔσεσθε ἐπίχαρμα τοῖς ἔθνεσι. (*Dial.* 72.)

Here, then, is the passage that we are in search of. It was in
Justin's *Testimony Book*, to be used against the Jews: and that
Lactantius wishes to use it for a similar anti-Judaic purpose, is
clear from his remark that "*the Jews* can clearly have no hope,
unless they wash off from them the blood of Christ, and hope in
Him whom they have denied." This is very like the capitulation
of Cyprian's closing chapter of his first book.

Quod solo hoc Judaei accipere veniam possint delictorum suorum, si
sanguinem Christi occisi baptismo eius abluerint et in ecclesiam transeuntes
praeceptis eius obtemperauerint.

Probably the disputed passage stood under this or a similar heading
in the Cyprianic archetype; it was removed, perhaps, because it
was not authentic: but if it was not a part of Ezra, it is to be
regarded as a part of the primitive *Testimony Book*, from whatever
source it was ultimately derived.

If we now look a line or two further on in Justin, we find him
complaining of the removal of a passage, which runs as follows:

Δεῦτε, ἐμβάλωμεν ξύλον εἰς τὸν ἄρτον αὐτοῦ καὶ ἐκτρίψωμεν αὐτὸν ἐκ γῆς
ζώντων, καὶ τὸ ὄνομα οὐ μὴ μνησθῇ οὐκέτι, i.e. Come, let us cast wood on his
bread, and expel him from the land of the living, and let his name be never
again remembered. (Jer. xi. 19.)

Justin wants to use this passage about "wood on the bread" (or
was it originally "bread on the wood?") as a prediction of Christ
on the Cross. His complaint of its removal was baseless: it is in
all copies of Jeremiah in the Septuagint. We notice that this
very same passage occurs in Lactantius a little lower down, and
it was actually quoted twice by Cyprian, in spite of the perverse-
ness of the involved exegesis (Cyp. *Test.* II. 20 and II. 15). The
coincidence in the treatment of the subject shows that all three
writers are working on a primitive Testimony. If Cyprian had

dropped it, we could have carried it back on the faith of Justin and Lactantius; he does not drop it because he knows it is in the Bible. Thus our confidence in the antiquity of the matters which are unexpectedly brought to light in Lactantius is heightened: the same thing comes out in other directions; for instance, though he seldom quotes the Gospels in this series of arguments, there seems to be no doubt that he has access to an early and uncanonical Gospel, perhaps the Gospel of Peter. He is a good source for the Christian antiquary to explore. Now what shall we say of the other expansion which Lactantius makes in the text of 1 Kings ix.? Is that part of an original Testimony?

Lactantius begins by saying that Solomon, the son of David, *who founded Jerusalem*, prophesied that the city should perish, in vengeance for the Holy Cross: then he quotes somewhat loosely 1 Ki. ix. 6—9.

If ye shall turn away from following me, etc. Why hath the Lord done this unto this land and to this house? And they shall answer, Because they forsook the Lord their God, and they *persecuted their King, most dear as he was to God, and they tortured him in great humility*: therefore hath the Lord brought all these evils upon them.

The words "persecuti sunt regem suum dilectissimum Deo, et cruciaverunt illum in humilitate magna," are an inset into the passage quoted, perhaps by way of a Christian commentary rather than as an expansion of the text. The whole passage is ancient in appearance, as the reference to the founding of Jerusalem by Solomon, or David, shows: such an error must, surely, be early; it survives, incidentally, in Lactantius as a monument of his fidelity to the tradition upon which he is working. We take the passage right back to the earliest strata of that tradition. So far, then, we see no reason to credit Lactantius with anything more than the re-iteration of Testimonies. If he shows matter in excess of what is exhibited to us in Cyprian, a closer examination will justify the additions on the ground of antiquity and prior patristic use of them in the sense in which Lactantius actually employs them.

It is, however, important for us to get some clearer idea of the extent of variation between the two types of collected Testimonies. Of the sixty-five citations in Lactantius there are thirteen not in Cyprian, all the others being sensibly in agreement.

Of these thirteen we note the following references:

Beatus qui erat antequam nasceretur: occurs as a testimony in Irenaeus, as we have shown above.

Ps. lxxxiii. (lxxxiv.) 11 occurs as a testimony in Irenaeus (*Mass.* 179).

Is. lxiii. 10, 11 occurs in Greg. Nyss. *Test.*

Is. xlv. 8 with a strange Arian reading which was almost sure to be discarded.

Is. xix. 20.

Ps. lxxi. (lxxii.) 6, 7 (the rain on the fleece) in Greg. Nyss.

Ps. xxxiv. (xxxv.) 15, 16.

Ps. lxviii. (lxix.) 21 in Greg. Nyss.

Ps. xciii. (xciv.) 21, 22.

1 Kings. The passage with the curious expansion.

Hosea xiii. 13 ff.

Jer. xii. 7, 8 (*dereliqui domum,* etc.)

and a famous passage from a lost Esdras, which occurs in Justin Martyr as we have shown above.

It will be seen that quite a number of the non-Cyprianic extracts from Lactantius can put in a claim to be genuine Testimonies, and not comments of Lactantius himself. We may therefore generalize the results of our inquiry and say that the citations of Lactantius which we have been examining are portions of an ancient tradition of *Testimonia adv. Judaeos.* This brings us to what is, perhaps, the most important point of all. In making our list and enumeration of the citations of Lactantius from the Old Testament (and it will be observed that he does not add New Testament citations, as Cyprian does, except one instance where he cites the Prologue to St John's Gospel), we left out of account the famous reference to the *Odes of Solomon,* which occurs in the very section upon which we are engaged. As is well known, Lactantius quotes some sentences which seem to refer to the Virgin Birth of Jesus from the 19th Ode of Solomon. The reference was important for the reconstruction and verification of the arrangement of the Odes in the recently discovered MS.; and it was naturally assumed that Lactantius had access to a Latin translation of the Odes in view of the fact that when he cites Greek authors like the Sibyl and Hermes, he makes his references to the original Greek. Apparently, then, he did not know a Greek text of the Odes. In view, however, of the investigation upon which we have been engaged and its probable results, we have to ask whether the famous passage from the Odes is not to be regarded, like the rest of the Biblical references of Lactantius, as a *Testimony*. So we turn to the text and the context and find as follows: Lactantius is undertaking to establish the Virgin Birth of Jesus *from the Prophets* (*de Jesu ortu ex Virgine*, de ejus Vita, Morte et Resurrectione: atque *de iis rebus testimonia Prophetarum*, according to the Editorial summary).

We see that Lactantius tells us at the beginning of the chapter that he is going to make an argument from the Testimonies of the Old Testament. He remarks that the Virgin Birth is not antecedently incredible, since even animals conceive from the wind[1] (it is a folklore belief, concerning mares, for example, to which he refers). If, however, we affirm that it is antecedently incredible, it would remain so if the Prophets had not long ago rehearsed the matter. That they did so is clear from the fact that Solomon says in his 19th Ode:

The womb of the Virgin became weak, and received a conception, and she became gravid, and in great mercy she became a mother.

Lactantius continues with a famous passage from Isaiah on the same subject, which he introduces thus:

Item propheta Esaias, cujus verba sunt haec.

The opening word (*item*) is the familiar term, which Lactantius (and Cyprian) employ when they pass from one member of a string of quotations to the next.

It is clear, therefore, that Lactantius cites the Odes as one of his collected *Testimonies*, and that, unless we are mistaken in our previous reasoning, this passage *was in the sources from which he was working, and was regarded as a part of the Old Testament.*

If this be the case, then the supposition which has prevailed that the Odes of Solomon were extant in a Latin Version in the time of Lactantius may be set on one side. *There is no evidence of any Latin Version at all.*

A Latin series of *Testimonies* is another thing altogether, and such a series depends, for certain, upon a previous Greek *Book of Testimonies*. The fact that the Odes of Solomon are not quoted by Cyprian does not militate against this. We have already seen that Cyprian modifies his collections; he probably would not have regarded the Odes as genuine Biblical matter.

---

[1] That the belief has lasted nearly to our own times, may be seen from the tract of John Hill, entitled *Lucina sine concubitu*.

If, however, we have weakened existing arguments for the antiquity of the Odes, drawn from the supposed existence of a Latin Version at the beginning of the fourth century, we have probably replaced the argument by a much stronger one. The original *Testimony Book* belongs, as we have shown in many ways, to the first age of the Church. The first traces of it that we discovered were anterior to Justin Martyr and Irenaeus, and it is to an early form of the document that we must refer the borrowed fragment of the Odes, and the fragment was borrowed by someone who imagined that he was quoting an Old Testament writer; otherwise he would not have incorporated the extract in a series of *Testimonies against the Jews*.

This does not necessarily mean that the Odes are a Jewish book. Writers who collect Testimonies were, as we have seen, under the temptation to parade non-Jewish and non-Biblical matter under the aegis of the Old Testament. Lactantius himself does this in his use of Christian Sibyls garbed as pagan, and, as we have intimated, Lactantius is by no means the first to take up seriously the literary fiction of Sibyls. Had not the Jews themselves done so, in Alexandria or elsewhere? When we practise a literary deception upon the public, they turn again and take us seriously. Enoch, though only a figure-head, becomes Enoch (even to Apostles) and Esdras Esdras, and Solomon Solomon. So we will leave the question of the ultimate authorship (Judaean or non-Judaean) of the Odes on one side for the moment; our contention is merely that they were, at a very early period of the Christian era, employed in a series of anti-Judaic Testimonies.

After writing the foregoing analysis, it comes to my notice that this is the same result that was announced by Pichon in his work on Lactantius, and was repeated by Bernard in his essay on the Odes of Solomon, as follows: "In Pichon's study of Lactantius, it is pointed out that his Bible quotations do not exhibit any special familiarity with the Old Testament—he only became a Christian while living in Nicomedia—and Pichon thinks he may have got them from a collection of *Testimonia* like Cyprian's...."

"The evidence, then, of Lactantius amounts to this—that the Odes were known and were ascribed to Solomon before the year 305 in the district of Nicomedia. We cannot be sure of the existence of a Latin Version, nor even whether Lactantius had access to them in Greek or in Syriac, but we can be sure that he accounted them to be genuine writings of Solomon."

We have shown that the *Testimony Book* used by Lactantius is something much earlier than the date when he made use of it, and that it can be carried back behind Cyprian and Justin. There is not the least probability of the passage from the Odes having been introduced into the book of prophetical citations in the fourth century[1].

[1] What Pichon really says is that the majority of the Biblical quotations of Lactantius are found in the *Testimonies* or elsewhere in the writings of Cyprian. When he comes to discuss those passages which Lactantius does not seem to have borrowed from Cyprian, he remarks that they almost all refer to the first Advent of Christ, or to the wrath of God against the Jews and the dissolution of the ancient Covenant. They serve to prove, either that Jesus is the Messiah, which the Jews deny, or that the Divine Wrath rests upon the Jewish people. They are therefore, Pichon suggests, borrowed from some polemical work against the Jews, in the style of Tertullian. But why multiply documents? It is precisely these points that are aimed at in the *Testimonies*. Pichon appears to forget that the *Testimonia* has a longer title, *Testimonia adversus Judaeos*, and that there is no reason to go further for a source from which Lactantius' quotations may be taken. Equally mistaken is the reference to *Tertullianus adversus Judaeos*, which is itself based upon the Testimony Book and a part of its tradition.

CHAPTER IX

The foregoing chapters have brought us to the conclusion that the early Christians made use of a manual of controversy in their disputes with the Jews which was composed of passages from the Old Testament arranged under appropriate headings, with brief introductory statements or accompanying comments.

Although I made the discovery, without the knowledge that other scholars had expressed similar suspicions, and had argued for the antiquity of the book, it was not the less pleasing to find that the late Dr Hatch and Professor Drummond had anticipated or endorsed me; for it furnished at once a confirmation and a check; it was a confirmation where we agreed, and suggested suspense of judgment and a revision of the argument where we differed. Recently the hypothesis has met with the support of Professor Burkitt, who has ventured the very bold conjecture that the primitive collection of Testimonies to which we are led was nothing more nor less than the lost book of *Dominical Oracles* of Papias. The matter, then, is certainly important enough to the critic, and the subject demands an exhaustive treatment. A wide area of patristic literature is involved in the investigation, with probably some publication or collation of fresh documents, and, perhaps, a re-collation of documents already known. These and kindred matters are reserved for Part II.

Meanwhile I have been assiduously following the traces of the lost book in the Fathers; it was natural that one should do this, in view of the fact that the first suspicions on the subject were provoked by the existence of curious coincidences in the texts of Justin and Irenaeus, both of whom can be now proved to have been intimately acquainted with the method of the *Testimony Book*, which, in one of its early forms, they had at their finger-ends.

From Justin and Irenaeus it was easy to work backwards, in search of the missing planet. Their coincidence in the treatment of prophetical matter could only be reasonably explained by allowing antiquity to the composition. But this brought one to the borders of New Testament times and necessitated an inquiry, which turned out to be very fruitful, into the influence of the early forms of the book upon Evangelists and Apostles. That the investigation has not been without results nor the arguments unconvincing may be inferred from the following sentences in Professor Gwatkin's recently published Church History :

> Vol. I. p. 199. "If they (the early Christian writers) were all borrowing from some very early manual of proof texts (Rendel Harris and Burkitt have this theory) which must be at least earlier than the First Gospel, we may safely say that few books have so influenced Christian thought."

We shall, I think, be able to show that Professor Gwatkin's statement does not over-estimate either the antiquity or the importance of the writing in question.

But what, to me at least, is as surprising as the demonstrable antiquity of the book, is its remarkable persistence, often with comparatively slight modifications, in the writings of later Fathers than Irenaeus and Justin from whom our inquiry started.

In the present chapter I am going to show that the *Testimony Book* was a part of the intellectual apparatus of no less a person than Athanasius, and that he drew upon it freely in his controversial works and in the public disputes into which he threw himself.

That something of the kind had affected him might have been suspected from the fact that he supported the doctrine of the Eternal Sonship, in his conflict with Arius, on a text from the 110th Psalm: "Before the day-star I begat thee." This argument did not originate with Athanasius; it is in Justin[1] and elsewhere, and a study of the sequences in which it occurs will prove that it came from the *Testimony Book*. It is, in fact, actually extant in Cyprian's *Testimonies*[2], in Gregory of Nyssa's *Testimonies against the Jews*[3] and in Bar Ṣalibi's tract on the same subject. So the suggestion arises whether Athanasius may not have been brought up on the same religious handbook as so many Fathers of the second century.

---

[1] *Dial.* 63.   [2] *Testim.* I. 18.   [3] *Loc. cit.* 292.

If we turn to Athanasius' treatise *On the Incarnation* we shall find that eight chapters (33—40) are occupied with a refutation of the unbelief of the Jews by means of arguments from the Prophets. Almost the first passage that he quotes is the prophecy of the Star in the Blessing of Jacob, which he introduces in the name of Moses:

And Moses also who was really great and was credited amongst the Jews as a true man, esteemed what was said of the incarnation of the Saviour as of great weight, and having recognized its truth he set it down, saying: There shall arise a star out of Jacob, and a man out of Israel, and he shall break the princes of Moab.

The point to notice is the intrusion of Moses into the argument, where he is awkwardly apologised for as not being the actual author but only the one who gave the passage its imprimatur; that this reference is not a mere accident may be seen by turning to a contemporary writer, Lactantius, who also quotes the prophecy:

De Div. Inst. IV. 13. And Moses also, in Numbers, thus speaks: There shall arise a star out of Jacob: and a man shall spring forth from Israel...

Athanasius and Lactantius agree, then, in the odd ascription of the prophecy to Moses.

It is easy to show (*vide supra* p. 10) that this passage, together with a companion text from Isaiah, stood in the *Testimony Book,* as known to Irenaeus and Justin; the primitive form was something like this:

Moses first prophesied: There shall come a star out of Jacob, etc.
And Isaiah: A flower shall spring out of the root of Jesse.

This passage suffered a displacement of title, and the whole of it was covered by the name Isaiah, as in Irenaeus and Justin. But the original form with 'Moses' persisted in other quarters, as we see in Athanasius and Lactantius.

In the next place, we find a second instance of the reference of prophecies in the Old Testament to Moses in the case of the Messianic prediction in the blessing of Jacob. For in the 40th chapter of Athanasius' treatise we have, in the ordinary texts, the following statement:

And Jacob prophesies that the Kingdom of the Jews should stand until this day, saying: A ruler shall not fail from Judah.

Examination of the authorities for the text shows that, according to the best MS. in the Bodleian library, we ought to read

And *Moses* prophesied, etc.

So here is another case of the direct ascription of an Old Testament prophecy to Moses. Is that a blunder on the part of Athanasius, or of some one who preceded him? Let us examine how Justin and Irenaeus quote the passage.

When we turn to Justin's *Apology*, c. 32, we find the following statement:

And Moses also, who was the first of the prophets, says expressly as follows: A ruler shall not fail from Judah, etc.

Moreover, we see that if this was a blunder on the part of Justin, it was a deliberate one; for, as we read his text a little further, we come to this:

It is your part, then, to examine accurately and to learn until whom the Jews had a ruler and a king of their own: it was until the manifestation of Jesus Christ, our teacher and the interpreter of the recognized prophecies, as was said aforetime by the holy and divine and *prophetical spirit through Moses.*

So it is clear that Justin was speaking deliberately when he put the famous Messianic prophecy into the mouth of Moses.

Let us see, in the next place, whether other people can be found making the same mistake. Irenaeus, for example, has a whole chapter in which he shows that Moses foretold the advent of Christ[1]. In the course of his argument he says that "Moses had already foretold his advent, saying, A ruler shall not fail, etc.," and ends up, in language very like that of Justin, "Let those look into the matter who are said to investigate everything, and let them tell us, etc."

Clearly Irenaeus has made the same mistake as Justin and had the matter in a somewhat similar setting. So Athanasius has simply repeated a blunder which was earlier than Justin and Irenaeus, and was probably found in the original book of proof-texts.

For further cases of the occurrence of the same mistake in Justin Martyr, we may take the following:

I. *Ap.* c. 54. Moses, then, the prophet, as we said before, was senior to all the chroniclers, and by him, as we previously intimated, the following prophecy was uttered: A ruler shall not fail, etc.

[1] Iren. lib. IV. c. 20.

In the *Dialogue with Trypho* he has found out the mistake and
tries to get rid of it, much as Athanasius does:

> *Dial.* c. 54. By Jacob the patriarch it was foretold, etc. That which was
> recorded by Moses, but prophesied by the patriarch Jacob, etc.
>   c. 76. Concerning whose blood also Moses spoke figuratively, that he
> should wash his robe in the blood of the grape,

where 'Moses' still stands uncorrected: a similar statement will be
found in c. 63.

We will now test Athanasius by seeing how he quotes the
prophecies in Isaiah xxxv. It will be remembered that these
passages in reference to the "lame man leaping like a hart" were
the starting-point for my inquiry, because it was found that both
Irenaeus and Justin had agreed in prefixing to the quoted prophecy
the words· "at His coming," ἐν τῇ παρουσίᾳ αὐτοῦ, the motive
for which was implicit in the previous verse:

> *Your God shall come* with vengeance, even God with a recompense. *He
> will come* and save you. Then (sc. at His coming) shall the lame man leap
> like an hart, etc.

Let us see, then, whether Athanasius knows anything of the
introductory words which Justin and Irenaeus took from their
Testimony Book. In c. 38 Athanasius quotes against the Jews
the words of Isaiah, beginning with "Be strong, ye relaxed hands
and paralysed knees," and continues the quotation down to "the
tongue of the stammerers shall be plain." Here then, is no sign of
the introductory comment, but as we read on, we find him saying
as follows:

> What then can the Jews say even on this point? And how can they dare
> even to face this statement? For the prophecy intimates *the arrival of God*,
> and makes known the signs and times *of His coming*, for they say that when
> the *Divine coming* takes place, the blind will see, etc.

Here the words on which we based an argument in the comparison
of Justin and Irenaeus, are found lurking in the context of
Athanasius. So we say again, in view of the quotation and the
involved comment, that Athanasius was using the *Book of Testimonies.*

It would be easy to point out further agreements in the order
and matter of prophecies quoted, but probably what has been said
will suffice. The case of Athanasius is important in view of his
central position in the teaching and life of the Church: he was

evidently little disposed to original treatment of Christian questions and much disposed to rearrange and slightly modify teaching which he had received in early life. And one is disposed to wonder whether this question of the Prophecies may not have been the principal factor in early Christian education; for we are gradually finding out that almost all the early Fathers have been learning out of the same book, and repeating the same arguments. Professor Gwatkin must be right in his statement as to the extraordinary influence of the text-book in question upon the development of the Christian religion.

In conclusion, it may not be out of place to add a few remarks in reference to Professor Burkitt's suggestion that we should identify the *Book of Testimonies* with the missing *Dominical Oracles* (Λόγια Κυριακά) of Papias. Assuming that the case has been made out for the influence of Testimonies on Athanasius' famous treatise on the Incarnation, let us see how he introduces the section in which he proposes to deal with the Jews, and in what terms he describes his material.

The opening section (c. 33) does not go beyond the statement that the Jews who disbelieve are confuted from their own Scriptures. In c. 37 he says that the Divine oracles (λόγοι) declare His generation to be ineffable. When, however, in c. 38, Athanasius brings forward a fresh batch of prophecies, he does so in the following terms:

If what has been said is not sufficient, let the Jews be persuaded from other oracles (λόγια) which are in their possession.

Here the very term is used which Papias has transmitted to us: and the language might be regarded as a direct confirmation of Professor Burkitt's hypothesis.

There is, however, one consideration which should be allowed weight on the other side. The very same prophecies which Athanasius proceeds to quote in c. 38 from the *Book of Testimonies* occur also in Justin's *Apology*[1] and we can compare the formula with which Justin introduces them: he says that

It has been foretold by Isaiah...that the Jews who have always been expecting Christ have failed to recognize Him when He came. And the sayings (λόγοι) were spoken as in the person of Christ Himself. They are as follows: "I was manifest to them that seek not after me."

[1] I. *Ap.* 49.

Here the identical prophecies which Athanasius calls *Logia* are called *Logoi* by Justin : as we have shown, Athanasius uses the terms interchangeably. So it will not do hastily to assign *Logia* to the prophecies of the Old Testament, and *Logoi* to the sayings of Jesus.

The terms are more nearly equivalent than are generally supposed; and the final decision on Professor Burkitt's hypothesis must be sought in other considerations.

CHAPTER X

THE ALTERCATION BETWEEN SIMON THE JEW
AND THEOPHILUS THE CHRISTIAN

The fifth-century writing *Altercatio Simonis et Theophili*, attributed to the authorship of Evagrius[1], is a member of an old line of anti-Judaic writings. Either directly or indirectly it is connected with the second-century *Controversy of Jason and Papiscus* that Ariston of Pella is said to have written. Questions of literary genealogy are, however, beyond our present purpose. What is significant is, that one of the chief evidences of ancient material in the dialogue is its use of *Testimonia*. That is to say, the writing has not only an old literary model of the Jason-and-Papiscus type, but also it uses the same theological source as its model uses. Moreover, its use of that source enables us to give body to a suggestion arising from the *Testimonia* of Cyprian, namely: that the extent of the Testimonies from which Cyprian drew must have been larger than his first two books. It would be natural, of course, for even a tiny collection of Testimonies, gathered with a polemical intent, to be the subject of increase by the natural expansion of the first polemical statements when they are used in actual controversy. But it becomes plain from the analysis of anti-Judaic writings that the *Book of Testimonies*, properly so called, was trimmed down by Cyprian. For example, there is an avoidance in his books of the subject of anti-Sabbatism; and thus the Cyprianic Testimonies are less in size than older documentary evidence would suggest for the collection. Or again, he extruded some things that Lactantius shows were in his edition of the *Testimonia*; and thus the books were smaller than a text of the polemical treatise would exhibit, say, in the middle of the second century. The *Altercatio* can make a contribution on this important matter of the expansions and contractions to which the *Book of Testimonies* was subject.

[1] Gennadius, *De Viris Illustribus*, 51; Marcellinus, *Chronicon*, ad ann. 423. Some scholars incline to the sixth century for the dating of the dialogue.

In Harnack's analysis of his text of the dialogue[1] he has reckoned that there are seventy-four agreements between Cyprian and the *Testimonies* of Evagrius. There are, indeed, seventy indubitable instances of agreement between the two writers out of about one hundred and thirty actual citations in Evagrius. Those instances, however, which are not to be found in Cyprian are, some of them, to be found in Justin; and what are not in Justin are in Novatian. As Justin receives much attention elsewhere, Novatian may be touched upon here.

The quotation of certain of the chapter headings from *De Trinitate* is sufficient to establish the fact that Novatian used the *Testimonia*. For instance:

c. XVIII. (*al.* XXVI.)[2] Inde etiam, quod Abrahae visus legatur Deus: quod de Patre nequeat intelligi, quem nemo vidit nunquam; sed de Filio in Angeli imagine.

c. XIX. (*al.* XXVII.) Quod etiam Jacob apparuerit Deus Angelus, nempe Dei Filius.

c. XX. (*al.* XV.) Ex Scripturis probatur, Christum fuisse Angelum appellatum. Attamen et Deum esse, ex aliis sacrae Scripturae locis ostenditur.

c. XXXI. Sed Dei Filium Deum, ex Deo Patre ab aeterno natum, qui semper in Patre fuerit, secundam personam esse a Patre qui nihil agat sine Patris arbitrio; eundem et Dominum, et Angelum magni Dei consilii; in quem Patris divinitas per substantiae communionem sit tradita.

The presence in the above of Testimony chapter headings together with theological concepts proper to them—though in this second feature Novatian is making them speak something of the language of his own time—is not to be doubted. Thus far Cyprian and Novatian come together. On the other hand, it might be shown by means of the *Testimonies* under the Novatian headings that the writer was drawing upon a larger scheme of Testimonies than Cyprian; but such a judgment would be based largely upon the argument from silence. It is probable that the deduction would be a valid one. A more positive method is to hand. It has been said that where Justin stops, as to coincidences with Evagrius in the use of Testimonies, Novatian goes on. Where there are genuine *Testimonia* chapter headings it will be natural to find equally genuine Testimonies. It is most unlikely that Novatian would interpolate a series of chapters reminiscent of

[1] Harnack, *Die Altercatio Simonis Judaei et Theophili Christiani*, 1883 (Texte und Unters. I. 3), 101.

[2] The second number refers to Pamelius' edition.

the ancient polemic to the degree of quoting its categories, and
that he should not quote matter from the polemic for which
its categories were framed. Concerning this it is to be noticed
under chapter xx. (xv.) Novatian cites Ps. lxxxii. 1 ff. and Ex. vii. 1
and the *Altercatio* quotes the passages in turn under i. 6 and ii. 7.
Now the introductory matter to the second Testimony in the
dialogue reads:

> Incredule Judaee, jam et de prophetis disputas? accipe tamen interroga-
> tioni tuae responsum. Deus ad Moysen loquitur dicens: "Ecce dedi te deum
> Pharaoni, et Aaron frater tuus erit tuus propheta." Pervide, hunc Moysen
> typum Christi fuisse, gentium incredibilium deum. Quanto magis Christus
> credentium est deus?[1]

The parallel from *De Trinitate* reads:

> Quae autem, malum, ratio est, ut cum legant hoc etiam Moysi nomen datum,
> dum dicitur: Deum te posui Pharaoni: Christo negetur, qui non Pharaoni
> Deus, sed universae creaturae et Dominus et Deus constitutus esse reperitur?

Both writers are evidently drawing from the same polemic
source; whether for context or citation they are possessors of a
larger common source than is represented in Cyprian. Further it
will be right to conclude that the original *Testimonia adversus
Judaeos* contained matter of a typological nature in the definition
of its Christology, for such matter was used in the *Epistle of
Barnabas* who is not independent of the traditional *Testimonia*[2].

---

[1] xx. *P. L.* 3. 926 c.

[2] Cf. the Ariston of Pella Fragment in Origen, *contra Celsum*, iv. 42: ἐν ᾧ
ἀναγέγραπται Χριστιανὸς Ἰουδαίῳ διαλεγόμενος ἀπὸ τῶν Ἰουδαϊκῶν Γραφῶν, καὶ δεικνὺς
τὰς περὶ τοῦ Χριστοῦ προφητείας ἐφαρμόζειν τῷ Ἰησοῦ· καὶ τοίγε οὐκ ἀγεννῶς
οὐδ' ἀπρεπῶς τῷ Ἰουδαϊκῷ προσώπῳ τοῦ ἑτέρου ἱσταμένου πρὸς τὸν λόγον. That
Testimonia were employed by Ariston is seen clearly from an introduction written
for a Latin translation of his work. Celsus, *Ad Vigilium ep. de Iudaica incredu-
litate*, e.g. cs. 4 and 6.

[V. B.]

CHAPTER XI

THE DIDASCALIA JACOBI

This curious tract which has been published in recent years in the *Oriental Patrology* gives a view of the arguments that commonly passed between the defenders of the Christian and Jewish positions respectively. The sub-title of the tract explains that it was written by a Jew who was baptized against his will in the time of Heraclius. Its date is 640 A.D. The time of its production depends on the edicts of Phocas in the first decade of the seventh century, when the order was given that all Jews should be baptized. After much travelling on land and much oscillation between the Greens and the Blues[1]—which colours were the signs of the alternately dominating political parties—the writer of the *Didascalia* reached Carthage where he was baptized. Most of these facts are contained in the tract. Nau, who is the editor of the Greek text[2], thinks that the writing is pseudepigraphic; and that the editor of the story lived either in Egypt or Syria because "his biblical citations agree constantly with the Egyptian Fathers." Other considerations tend to the belief that what is distinctive in the biblical text of the *Didascalia* belongs to the Greek *Testimony Book* and, therefore, furnishes no hint of the locality of the author. To establish the presence of *Testimonies* in this writing it will be enough to take the sections dealing with the "Passion of Christ foretold" and His "Death and Resurrection[3]." One small group is represented in the text of the *Testimonia* known to Evagrius, which, as we have seen in a previous chapter, is another way of saying "the text of the *Testimonia* known to Cyprian and Justin." These are striking facts in the light of Nau's conclusion. An analysis of the citations yields the following results:

A. *Didascalia*: (a) Is. lii. 13–15; (b) liii. 3–5; (c) Zech. xii. 10; (d) Gen. xlix. 9; (e) Num. xxiv. 8; (f) Ps. cvi. 20, 13–16; (g) Is. liii. 8–9; (h) Is. xlix.

---

[1] *Didasc. Jac.* 53.
[2] *Patr. Or.* VIII. 713 ff.; the Ethiopic Version is in *Patr. Or.* III. 556 ff.
[3] 26–28.

9; (*i*) Ps. lxxviii. 8–9; (*j*) Ps. xliii. 27, 24; (*k*) Ps. lxvii. 2, 19; (*l*) Nah. ii. 7–8; (*m*) Is. ix. 2; (*n*) Is. lvii. 1, 2; (*o*) Is. liii. 12; (*p*) Jer. xi. 19:

of which there are found in

B.   Cyprian, *Test.*: (*a*) omits; (*b*) II. 13; (*c*) II. 20; (*d*) I. 21; (*e*) II. 10; (*f*) II. 3; (*g*) II. 13; (*h*) omits to (*l*); (*m*) I. 21; (*n*) II. 14; (*o*) II. 13; (*p*) II. 15;

and there are the following coincidences with

C.   Justin: (*a*) I. *Ap.* 50 and *Tryph.* 118. 4; (*b*) throughout *Tryph.* from 14. 8 to 137. 1; (*c*) I. *Ap.* 52 and *Tryph.* 32. 2; (*d*) I. *Ap.* 32. 54; and cf. *Tryph.* 52. 2, 120; (*e*) cf. *Tryph.* 106. 4; (*f*) *Tryph.* 66. 1; (*g*) I. *Ap.* 51 and *Tryph.* 43, 63, 68, 76, 89, 97, 102, 110; (*h*) cf. *Tryph.* 121. 4, 122. 5; (*i*) to (*l*) omit as Cyprian; (*m*) I. *Ap.* 35, and *Tryph.* 86. 4 and 86. 3; (*n*) *Tryph.* 16. 4, 97. 2, 110. 6, 118. 1, 119. 3; (*o*) I. *Ap.* 51 and *Tryph.* 89. 3, 110. 2; (*p*) *Tryph.* 72. 2–3.

The series of quotations from the Psalter will be found to be represented by

D.   *Altercatio*, VI. 25.

Whether, then, Cyprian or Justin or Evagrius be regarded, the presence of the *Testimony Book* is demonstrated.

In the second place, the real peculiarities of Jacob's text, or, as we must more rightly name it, his *Testimonia* text, are on the surface in exact agreement with what looks like Justin's Bible. To test this matter we may range over the whole of the *Didascalia*.

	Didascalia.	Justin, *Trypho.*
12.	Is. xlii. 1–4; καὶ κρίσιν, οὐ κατεάξει.	123. 8.
16.	Is. xl. 3–5; εἰς ὁδοὺς λείας.	50. 3.
21.	Is. xxix. 13, 14; τὴν σοφίαν τῶν σοφῶν αὐτῶν.	78. 11.
30. and 43.	Jer. xi. 19; ἐκ γῆς ζώντων.	72. 2.
35.	Micah iv. 1; ἔσται ἐπ᾽ ἐσχάτου.	109. 2.
50.	Gen. xxix. 16 and epitomises argument of Leah and Rachel as Synagogue and Church	134. 3 f.

The last reference has been made with the intention of showing that the coincidences with Justin involved something more than textual agreements: the Leah and Rachel subject appears, for instance, in Commodian[1] where he says "Inspice Liam, typum Synagogae fuisse." Dombart has shown the influence of the *Testimony Book* on this third-century Latin poet as it is seen in his other work, the *Carmen Apologeticum*. Hence Jacob need not have been in direct dependence upon Justin. Another illustration

[1] *Instructiones*, XXXIX. *P. L.* 5. 230 A.

of this kind is in the parallel between the *Didascalia* and *Trypho* where they have:

D. xlv.: καὶ Μωϋσῆς δὲ, ξύλον βαλὼν εἰς Μερρὰν καὶ εἰς τὰ πικρὰ ὕδατα, ἐγλύκανεν αὐτὰ εἰς τύπον τοῦ σταυροῦ τοῦ Χριστοῦ.

T. lxxxvi. 1: καὶ ξύλον βαλὼν εἰς τὸ ἐν Μερρᾷ ὕδωρ, πικρὸν ὄν, γλυκὺ ἐποίησε.

lxxxvi. 6: διὰ τοῦ σταυρωθῆναι ἐπὶ τοῦ ξύλου καὶ δι' ὕδατος.

If it is shown that the above is a Testimony and not a literary parallel, the notion of Jacob's borrowing from Justin can again be discounted. On turning to the *Catecheses*[1] by Cyril of Jerusalem, he is found saying: τὸ ξύλον ἐπὶ Μωϋσέως ἐγλύκανε τὸ ὕδωρ. Cyril makes this allusion when writing on the same doctrinal matter as Evagrius; and also uses exactly the same verb as he. Further, this usage is in a series of chapters teeming with actual *Testimonia*. In the preceding chapter to the one we have quoted[2] Cyril makes use in succession of the notable "wood on his bread" passage, and the old Testimony name for Jesus, Life; καὶ ὅτι γε ζωὴ ἦν ἡ ἐπὶ τοῦ ξύλου κρεμασθεῖσα, and quotes Deut. xxviii. 66. This is the order of Cyprian, *Test.* II. 20. The second passage opens c. VII. in Gregory of Nyssa's tract. And the Testimony order for the two passages is maintained by Lactantius, *Div. Inst.* IV. 18. Reverting to the thirteenth chapter of Cyril it should be noticed that the remaining Old Testament citations are probably drawn from the missing typological sections of the *Book of Testimonies*. Further afield than this we do not go here, to prove Cyril's use of the ancient polemical book. He has served to demonstrate that there was a Greek version of the *Testimony Book* which, from readings preserved in Justin and Evagrius, can be shown to have distinctive features in its biblical text.

Thus some are in a Roman writing, since Justin belongs there rather than to Samaria or Ephesus; and some are in the Carthaginian *Didascalia*, supposing the geographical inference to hold and discarding Nau's idea of an Egyptian biblical base.

---

[1] xiii. 20.　　　　　　[2] xiii. 19.

[V. B.]

CHAPTER XII

We have given in the previous pages the proofs of the antiquity
and wide diffusion of the collection of prophecies employed by the
early Christians in their controversies with the Jews. We have
seen reason to believe that it was to some extent fluid, and that it
was accommodated at various points to the needs of the time, and
subject to some change, under hostile criticism or closer study.
Thus some peculiar *Testimonies*, no doubt, disappeared. The
Jews said they were not in the sacred text, and the Christians, after
first suggesting that, in that case, the Jews had themselves removed
them, after a while themselves withdrew the contested matter.
Occasionally a discarded Testimony flamed up into new life in the
Church itself, as when Venantius Fortunatus wrote the *Vexilla
regis* and gave us the lines

> Among the nations, God, saith he,
> Hath reigned and triumphed from the tree.

When controversy with the Jews died down, the Testimonies
became, as we have shown, a handbook of Christian doctrine;
and this change turned nearly all the first book of the Cyprianic
proofs, which are occupied with the idolatry and unfaithfulness of
the Jews, into waste paper. By this time, too, Christian doctrine
had become so much more highly developed at the hands of the
great Councils and the great Councillors, that it no longer sufficed
to bring forward proofs that Christ was the Logos, or the Arm of
God, or the Stone of Daniel. We see the change in the collection
of Testimonies ascribed to Gregory of Nyssa: where the opening
sections are now concerned directly with the doctrine of the
Trinity, in a more advanced form than the first Testimony men
had suggested. And it seems clear that this process of change
must have continued, as long as there were fresh factors to be
emphasized in the Christology or new heresies to be contradicted

in Scripture terms. We have no means of tracing the decay of the *Testimony Book* in detail, nor of determining when it passed into permanent disuse. We have shown that in Mesopotamia it had by no means lost its original form in the twelfth century. In the west it is more difficult to trace the rate of decline and of disappearance. The latest case of the Greek *Testimony Book* that we have come across appears to be as late as the invention of printing, or perhaps even later, as we shall now proceed to demonstrate.

There is in the monastery of Iveron on Mount Athos a paper MS., which Prof. Lambros in his catalogue assigns to the sixteenth century, filled with all kinds of theological extracts.

Amongst these multitudinous scraps I find as follows, according to Lambros' description, on which I make running comments, reserving the text for further study,

Cod. 4508 (=388), § 120 (f. 469 vᵒ). Ματθαίου μονάχου· Συγγραφὴ κατὰ Ἰουδαίων ἀνεπίγραφος· ἐν λόγοις εʹ. λόγος αʹ. (f. 469 vᵒ) ἀνεπίγραφος.

Note in passing that the work which is to follow is a work against the Jews in five books. It is said to be ἀνεπίγραφος, but this does not mean that it has no author's name: for

(1) the author is said to be Matthew the Monk;

(2) the first book is like the whole treatise ἀνεπίγραφος;

clearly this is Lambros' way of saying that there is no summary or description prefixed.

The first book is divided into four chapters as follows:

κεφ. αʹ. ὅτι τριυπόστατον καὶ ἡ πάλαια τὸν Θεὸν κηρύττει Γραφὴ ἐν πατρὶ καὶ υἱῷ καὶ ἁγίῳ πνεύματι προσκυνούμενον.

κεφ. βʹ. ὅτι οὐ μόνον Κύριος καὶ Θεὸς ἀλλὰ καὶ ἄγγελος ὁ τοῦ Θεοῦ υἱὸς παρὰ τῇ παλαιᾷ καλεῖται Γραφῇ.

The reader will have already been struck by the fact that he has before him a series of demonstrations against the Jews *from the Old Testament* as to the nature of the Trinity, and will recall what was said above as to the replacement of the first chapters of the *Testimony Book* by a section on the Trinity in the collection of Gregory of Nyssa.

It will also at once arrest attention that the second chapter is concerned to prove that the Son of God is not only *God and Lord* but that He is also called *Angel* in the Old Testament. For we remember that the second book of Cyprian's *Testimonies* has for its fifth chapter the statement

Quod idem angelus et deus.

Nor need we have any doubt as to the antiquity of the proof that Christ is also called Angel, since we have the same ascription in Justin's *Dialogue with Trypho* (c. 126) where we find him asking,

> Who is this who sometimes is called the *Angel of Great Counsel*, and by Ezekiel is called a man, and by Daniel one like to the Son of Man, etc. etc.?

So in c. 34 we are told that

> Christ is called King and Priest and God and Lord and *Angel* and Man and Commander-in-Chief, and Stone and Child Born (to us) and the One that was passible ($\pi\alpha\theta\eta\tau\delta s$) at his first advent, etc.

We need not multiply quotations to prove that Christ was the Angel in Justin's *Testimony Book*. So the matter in the Athos MS. is primitive, as far as the Angel is concerned.

The term "angel" which Monk Matthew gives to Christ, and which we recognize to be Cyprianic and Justinian, is interesting as being one of the titles of the Messiah discovered in the Old Testament and subsequently discarded. The reason of this abandonment of what was certainly one of the leading heads of Testimony lay in the fact that another proof-text, upon which great stress was laid, stated that it was "not an elder, nor an angel, but the Lord Himself who saved us" (Is. lxiii. 9). Thus Christ was the Angel and not an angel! To avoid the perplexity caused by this contradiction, it seems that the angel proof-text was abandoned, and the other one preserved. At first they stood in the same document and almost side by side. Cyprian, for example, has them both. It is clear, at all events, that Monk Matthew is handling very early traditions. The following remark from Harnack's *History of Dogma* will put the case for us:

> Angel is a very old designation for Christ (see Justin's *Dial.*) which maintained itself up to the Nicaean controversy and is expressly claimed for Him in Novatian's treatise *De Trinitate* (II. 25 ff.). *The word was taken from Old Testament passages which applied to Christ*...From the earliest times we find this idea contradicted...yet it never got the length of a great controversy, and as the Logos doctrine gradually made way, the designation 'Angel' became harmless and then vanished. (Harnack, *l. c.* I. 185 n. Eng. tr.)

The MS. proceeds:

> κεφ. γ´. ὅτι προαιωνίως γεγεννῆσθαι τὸν υἱὸν ἐκ τοῦ πατρὸς καὶ ἡ παλαιὰ δογματίζει Γραφὴ καὶ συναΐδιον τῷ Πατρὶ καὶ τῷ ἁγίῳ Πνεύματι καὶ τῆς κτίσεως συνδημιουργόν.

This is the opening section of the second book of Cyprian's *Testimonies*:

Christum primogenitum esse et ipsum esse sapientiam Dei, per quem omnia facta sunt.

κεφ. δ'. περὶ τῆς ἀρρήτου προαιωνίου τοῦ υἱοῦ ἐκ τοῦ πατρὸς γεννήσεως.

This is really a repetition, or subsection, of the previous chapter. Both chapters depend ultimately on Proverbs viii.:

viii. 23.   πρὸ τοῦ αἰῶνος ἐθεμελίωσέν με.

viii. 25.   πρὸ δὲ πάντων βουνῶν γεννᾷ με.

The writer, or his archetype, has actually made out of πρὸ τοῦ αἰῶνος an adjective προαιώνιος and a corresponding adverb. There can be no doubt as to the origin of the proofs that are here adduced against the Jews.

The second book (f. 473 vᵒ) has a special heading in the form of a question as to why in the beginning only God the Father was expressly proclaimed, and why the Holy Spirit is more slightly referred to than the Son:

Διατὶ μόνος ἀπ' ἀρχῆς διαρρήδην ὁ Θεὸς καὶ πατὴρ ἐκηρύττετο, καὶ διατὶ τὸ ἅγιον πνεῦμα γυμνώτερον ὠνομάζετο ἢ ὁ Υἱός......

Then follows the opening of the book, which appears to consist of a single chapter. It runs as follows:

Seeing that the nature of the three persons in the Godhead is one and unchangeably the same, and likewise they are equal in Glory and Counsel and Power and Energy, why was only God the Father openly proclaimed at first by the Law and the Prophets?

Διατί, μιᾶς οὔσης καὶ ἀπαραλλάκτου τῆς φύσεως τῶν τριῶν τῆς θεαρχίας προσώπων ὥσπερ δὴ καὶ τῆς δόξης καὶ τῆς βουλῆς καὶ τῆς δυνάμεως καὶ τῆς ἐνεργείας, μόνος τὸ πρῶτον ὁ Θεὸς καὶ πατὴρ διά τε νόμου καὶ προφητῶν ἐκηρύττετο ἐμφανῶς.

The third book (f. 477 vᵒ) deals, for the most part, with the Incarnation. Apparently there is no special introduction. The chapters are as follows:

κεφ. α'. περὶ τῆς ἐνσάρκου τοῦ Θεοῦ λόγου οἰκονομίας.

The chapter seems to contain general predictions of the Incarnation.

κεφ. β'. πρὸς τοὺς μὴ πιστεύοντας ὅτι τέτοκεν ἡ παρθένος.

The chapter discusses the Virgin Birth, with the view of confuting those who do not believe it.

We naturally expect that the foundation of the argument would be the famous passage of Isaiah, "Behold! a virgin shall conceive," as we find in Justin, I. *Ap.* 33, in Cyp. *Test.* II. 9, Lact. *Inst.* IV. 12, and Athan. *De Incarn.* 33, all of whom are working from the *Testimony Book.* It is, however, worth while to look a little closer into the matter, on account of the contradictory manner into which the summary of the chapter is thrown; it is described as "against those *who do not believe* the Virgin Birth." Let us turn to Justin's words in the introduction of the subject: he tells us, "Now listen again how expressly it was foretold by Isaiah, that He should be born of a Virgin; for thus it was said: Behold a Virgin etc. For the things which seemed to be *unbelievable* and which are reckoned impossible to occur amongst men, these things God intimated in advance by the Spirit of Prophecy that they were going to occur, in order that when they did occur *they should not be disbelieved, but should be believed* on account of their having been foretold."

Here we see Justin in agreement with Matthew the Monk, in rebutting the incredulity of those who say that the Virgin Birth is incredible.

κεφ. γ΄. περὶ τοῦ καιροῦ τῆς τοῦ χριστοῦ παρουσίας.

The time of Christ's coming is usually argued by the early writers in connexion with the passing away of the sceptre from Judah. Probably that is the line taken in our MS. The proof of the "time" was usually accompanied by an identification of the "place," as in Cyp. *Test.* II. 12, where Micah v. 2 is, of course, the proof-text.

κεφ. δ΄. ὅτι θεὸν ἀληθῆ τὸν χριστὸν ἡ θεία κηρύττει Γραφή.

Apparently this corresponds to Cyp. *Test.* II. 6,

Quod Deus Christus.

κεφ. ε΄. Διατὶ μὴ ὁ πατὴρ ἢ τὸ πνεῦμα τὸ ἅγιον ἐσαρκώθη.

The question as to why it was the Son that was incarnate and not the Father nor the Holy Spirit, appears to belong to a later deposit of tradition.

The fourth book has again no introductory matter: its first chapter is (f. 484 recto):

κεφ. α΄. ὅτι νομοθέτην ἡ Γραφὴ τὸν χριστὸν ἔσεσθαι προεθέσπισε πολιτείας ὑψηλοτέρας.

The statement that Christ was to be the Lawgiver of a loftier state, in spite of its rhetorical embellishment, does not seem to be anything different from the proofs in the first book of Cyprian's *Testimonies* (I. 9—11)

Quod lex prior quae per Moysen data est cessatura esset. Quod lex nova dari haberet. Quod dispositio alia et testamentum novum dari haberet.

κεφ. β΄. περὶ θυσιῶν καὶ τίς ἡ ἀληθὴς καὶ εὐπρόσδεκτος τῷ Θεῷ θυσία.

It is easy to infer that this is only a variation of Cyp. *Test.* I. 16

Quod sacrificium vetus evacuaretur et novum celebraretur.

κεφ. γ΄. περὶ περιτομῆς καὶ τίς ἡ ἀληθὴς περιτομή.

We should compare Cyp. *Test.* I. 8:

Quod circumcisio prima carnalis evacuata sit et secunda spiritalis repromissa sit.

The chapter on circumcision is followed by one on the keeping of the Sabbath:

κεφ. δ΄. περὶ σαββάτου καὶ τῶν λοιπῶν νομικῶν παρατηρήσεων.

The best comment on these sections will perhaps be Justin, *Dial.* 12,

There was need of a *second* circumcision and ye swagger over a circumcision of the flesh; the *new law* bids you to keep sabbath always, and you think that by idling a single day you have become pious.

The second circumcision has its proof-text in Joshua v. 2, 3.

The fifth book of Matthew's treatise is again without superscription: it is introduced as follows:

(f. 484 v°) κεφ. α΄. περὶ τῆς τῶν ἐθνῶν κλήσεως.

Apparently this answers to Cyprian's section on the superiority of the Gentiles to the Jews in *Test.* I. 21:

Quod gentes magis in Christum crediturae essent.

The early testifiers have naturally an abundance of references on this point.

The next chapter is concerned with the sufferings of the Messiah.

κεφ. β΄. ὅτι τὸ κατὰ σάρκα παθεῖν τὸν χριστὸν ἡ θεία Γραφὴ σαφῶς προεκήρυξεν.

The question as to whether Christ is παθητὸς is alluded to in the Acts of the Apostles, and it is one of Justin Martyr's special points: one need not refer to the proof-texts which are obvious, but the references to Justin may again be taken:

Dial. 52. And by Jacob the patriarch it was foretold that there would be two advents of Christ, and *that with the first advent he would be passible* (παθητός).

The next chapter reverts to the rejection of the Jews, and finds its obvious parallel in Cyprian and elsewhere:

κεφ. γ΄. ὅτι οὐδὲν ὄφελος τοῖς Ἰουδαίοις ἡ τῆς θείας Γραφῆς ἀνάγνωσις μὴ πιστεύσασιν εἰς χριστόν.

Cyp. *Test.* I. 5. *Nihil posse Judaeos intellegere de Scripturis, nisi prius crediderunt in Christum.*

κεφ. δ΄. ὅτι ἡ συναγωγὴ τῶν Ἰουδαίων καὶ εἰδωλείου χείρων εἰς ἀκαθαρσίαν καθέστηκεν.

This appears to mean that a Jewish synagogue is a worse centre of impurity than an idol-temple.

κεφ. ε΄. ὅτι τὸ ἐκτὸς τῶν Ἱεροσολύμων τολμᾶν τοὺς Ἰουδαίους τινὰ τῶν παλαιῶν νομίμων ἐπιτελεῖν οὐδεμίαν παρανομίαν ὑπερβολῆς (l. παρανομίας ὑπερβολὴν) καταλείπει.

It is the acme of impiety for the Jews to try and keep up their ritual outside of Jerusalem.

This appears to be based on those Testimonies which emphasize the removal of the Jews from the Holy City: perhaps the nearest parallels are:

Cyp. *Test.* I. 6. Quod Hierusalem perdituri essent, etc.

Just. *Apol.* I. 47. εἴρηται δὲ καὶ περὶ τῆς ἐρημώσεως αὐτῆς καὶ περὶ τοῦ μὴ ἐπιτραπήσεσθαι μηδένα αὐτῶν οἰκεῖν.

κεφ. δ΄. ὅτι διὰ τὴν κατὰ τοῦ χριστοῦ μανίαν καὶ ἐξορίᾳ διηνεκεῖ καὶ ἡ προφητικὴ χάρις ἀπεσβέσθη.

This section, as to their perpetual exile, and the loss of their prophetical gifts, is closely connected with the previous chapter. The Cyprianic sequence is

Test. I. 6. *Quod Hierusalem perdituri essent et terram quam acceperant relicturi.*

I. 7. *Item quod essent amissuri lumen Domini.*

For the cessation and transfer of the prophetic gifts, we have plenty of evidence in the Testimony writers. Thus Justin, *Dial.* 82 says:

Amongst us Christians there are till the present time prophetic charismata, and from that you ought to infer that the gifts which were formerly yours have now been transferred to us.

Bar Ṣalibi also (§ 14) has a curious note in his tract against the Jews, when he turns to ask them whether it was man's doing that they had lost the *grace of prophecy,* the fire from heaven, the Bath Kol, the bubbling of the sacred oil, and the sparkling of the gems in Aaron's breastplate.

The next chapter in Monk Matthew is concerned with the doctrine of the *Two Advents* of Christ:

κεφ. ζ΄. ὅτι δύο τὰς παρουσίας ἡ θεία Γραφὴ κηρύττει τοῦ χριστοῦ, καὶ δύο προδρόμους Ἰωάννας (sic) καὶ Ἠλίας (sic).

The importance of the doctrine of the *Two Advents* in the *Testimony Book* will hardly need to be emphasized. Justin tells the Roman senate in his *Apology* (c. 52) as follows:

> The prophets foretold two advents of His; one has already occurred, the advent of a dishonoured and passible (παθητός) man; the second, when (as it has been proclaimed) He shall come in glory from Heaven along with the Angelic hosts.

Then follow the prophetic Testimonies which Justin has in mind, and which, no doubt, were in his handbook. It is not a mere expansion on the part of the monk Matthew that we find here a curious reference to the two precursors of the two advents; Justin makes in his *Dialogue* the very same connexion:

> *Dial.* c. 49. I asked him (Trypho) again and said:
> Does not the Word (λόγος) affirm by Zachariah (Malachi i.) that Elias was to come before the great and terrible day of the Lord?
> Certainly, he replied.
> If then, the Word compels us to admit that two Advents of the Messiah were foretold, one in which he was to appear passible and dishonourable and uncomely, the other in which he will come glorious and as the Judge of all (as I have already demonstrated at some length), ought we not to understand that the Word of God has proclaimed that Elias will be the precursor of the second Advent?
> Very true, said he.
> Then, said I,...the herald of his past manifestation is the spirit which aforetime came in Elias, and now in John, etc.

Thus the very same connexion between the two advents and the two precursors is made by Justin Martyr and by Matthew the Monk. The same sequence is found in Greg. Nyss. *Testim.* c. 17

ὅτι πρὸ τῆς τοῦ κυρίου δευτέρας παρουσίας ἐλεύσεται Ἠλίας.

The next three chapters appear to belong to a later period than the time in which the first book of *Testimonies* was collected. They relate to the nature of the devil, and to the problem as to why God did not become an incarnate Angel on behalf of the angels, as He became Man for the sake of men.

Then follows a new section, concerning which Lambros is in doubt as to whether it belongs to the same treatise. It opens as follows:

κεφ. α΄. ὁ πατριάρχης Ἰακὼβ τὸν ἐξ Ἰούδα ἐλευσόμενον βασιλέα χριστὸν προσδοκίαν εἶπεν εἶναι τῶν ἐθνῶν,

and it is said that in this chapter there are fragments from the Fathers. As far as the transcript goes it seems clear that we are dealing with one of the most famous of all prophetic Testimonies, perhaps selected from the foregoing for special treatment.

To sum up our inquiry:

Whatever the Athos MS. may contain in the way of proofs of its various theses, there can be no doubt that the majority of the theses are directly descended from the primitive collections of the first and second centuries; so that the MS. may be regarded as the latest of the *Testimony Books*.

Now this raises a very interesting question; who is Matthew the Monk? he does not seem to be known elsewhere in the ecclesiastical literature. We have shown that he is little more than a compiler or an editor working on a compilation. Is it possible that the original form of the tradition contained the name of Matthew, and that the quality of "monk" is of later addition? If that could be maintained, we should then say that the original author of the *Book of Testimonies* was Matthew the Apostle. We have already carried the book so far back into Christian antiquity as to make its first form earlier than almost every book of the New Testament. It follows, almost of a certainty, that its author was a member of the Apostolic company. Why not Matthew? The objection appears to be that if these *Testimonies* are the *Dominical Oracles* which Matthew wrote, they should have been written originally in the Hebrew (or Aramaic) language; but it seems quite clear that we have been working frequently on the Septuagint, even in defiance of the Hebrew. This is a very strong objection and needs further consideration.

On the other hand, note that our author, as he appears in his latest dress, is divided into *five books*. We remember that Papias wrote *five books* on the *Dominical Oracles*; now whatever these Oracles were, sayings of Jesus or words of the Prophets about Jesus, *five books of commentary imply five books of underlying text.* Is it a mere coincidence that we find five such books extant in the Athos MS.? and ascribed to Matthew?

In the conjunction of an author named Matthew with five such books, have we not gone a long way towards establishing Prof. Burkitt's conjecture[1] that the *Book of Testimonies* is the missing *Dominical Oracles* written by Matthew and commented on by Papias?

Is there any way to clear the matter up? Are we, perhaps, nearer to the solution?

Prefixed to the section that we have been discussing from the Athos Codex are the following Greek verses:

Ματθαῖος εἴργει τῶν Ἰουδαίων θράσος
Ὥσπερ χαλινοῖς πέντε φιμώσας λόγοις·
Ὅστις δὲ τούτων τὴν ἐπίρρητον πλάνην,
Πλάνην ἀτέχνως, ἐξελέγξει τῷ λόγῳ,
Ἄρδην ἁπάσας συγκαθεῖλεν αἱρέσεις.
Μήτηρ γὰρ αὐτῶν ἡ θεοκτόνων ἔρις.

Now this is not poetry of the first order, but it is certainly not mediaeval verse; it is, for instance, very much better than the memorial verses which we find in the Menaea or Synaxaria of the Greek Church. I suspect the person who wrote them really thought he was honouring a person of distinction, and that he was doing it in a distinguished manner. He was not a monk lauding a monk. Certainly the style of the writing is somewhat superior to that in which an ancient presbyter, quoted by Irenaeus, attacks the πλάνη of the Gnostic Marcus:

Εἰδωλοποιέ, Μάρκε, καὶ τερατοσκόπε,
Ἀστρολογικῆς ἔμπειρε καὶ μαγικῆς τέχνης,
Δι' ὧν κρατύνεις τῆς πλάνης [τὰ] διδάγματα,
Σημεῖα δεικνὺς τοῖς ὑπό σου πλανωμένοις,
Ἀποστατικῆς δυνάμεως ἐγχειρήματα,
Ἅ σοι χωρηγεῖ σὸς πατὴρ Σατανᾶς ἀεὶ
Δι' ἀγγελικῆς δυνάμεως Ἀζαζὴλ ποιεῖν
Ἔχων σε πρόδρομον ἀντιθέου πανουργίας.

There are, however, some slight similarities: there is the recurrence of the idea of πλάνη in two successive lines; and there is the parallel in the last line between the ἀντίθεος πανουργία and the θεοκτόνων ἔρις.

The two sets of verses are, as we shall presently see, not very different in date. The author of the verses quoted by Irenaeus is, almost certainly, Pothinus, his predecessor in the care of the church at Lyons.

[1] *Gospel History and its Transmission*, 126, 127.

Let us examine these verses more closely which are here prefixed to the books of Matthew against the Jews. We are told in the last line that "the strife of the Deicide people is the mother of all later heresies." The writer has already explained the importance of the refutation of the Jews: refute them, and you refute the heresies which spring from them. It is now expressly stated in an epigrammatic line that all the heresies which the Church has to confute spring from Jewish influence and Jewish methods of interpretation; and perhaps the term "Jewish strife" may include more than Jewish hostility to Christianity and cover Jewish divisions or schools of thought, for it is not easy to see why Jewish hostility, as such, should be the parent of Christian heresies. We shall assume tentatively that Christian heresies are a pendant to Jewish heresies.

Without making such an assumption, however, we can see that such a statement as we are discussing can hardly be the product of an unknown monk's reflections at some late period in the Church's history. So we naturally inquire whether there was in the Early Church any sentiment that corresponds with what we here find versified.

Now if we were to turn to Harnack's *History of Dogma* (Eng. tr. I. 243) we shall find the following illuminating sentence:

We find in Hegesippus, one of the earliest writers on the subject (of heresy), that the whole of the heretical schools sprang out of Judaism or the Jewish sects; in the later writers, Irenaeus, Tertullian, and Hippolytus, that these schools owe most to the doctrines of Pythagoras, Plato, Aristotle, Zeno, etc.

It is clear that, since the writings of Hegesippus were well known to the Fathers who followed him (as for instance to Hippolytus), that there has been some change of opinions amongst early ecclesiastical writers as to the dependence of the early heresies upon Jewish thought; and we infer that the versifier of our MS. depends upon the stratum of Christian thought represented by Hegesippus. It may even be an earlier stratum that is carried on from Hegesippus to a later date by tradition; we are at least justified in saying that our poet deals with early matter when he says "Jewish thought is the parent of Christian heresy."

Now let us turn to Hegesippus and see what he actually does tell us on the matter of the origin of heresies. We naturally approach the subject with some scepticism; perhaps we are saying to ourselves that, while it may be possible to give Jewish roots to some forms of Gnosticism, such a great heresy as Marcionism must be fundamentally anti-Judaic. Let us then get to Hegesippus himself.

The fundamental passage will be found in Eusebius as follows:

ἀπὸ τῶν ἑπτὰ αἱρέσεων καὶ αὐτὸς [sc. Θέβουθις] ἦν ἐν τῷ λαῷ· ἀφ' ὧν Σίμων, ὅθεν οἱ Σιμωνιανοί· καὶ Κλεόβιος, ὅθεν Κλεοβιηνοί· καὶ Δοσίθεος, ὅθεν Δοσιθεανοί· καὶ Γορθαῖος, ὅθεν Γορθηωνοί· καὶ Μασβώθεος, ὅθεν Μασβωθαῖοι· ἀπὸ τούτων Μενανδριανισταί, καὶ Μαρκιωνισταί, καὶ Καρποκρατιανοί, καὶ Οὐλεντινιανοί, καὶ Βασιλειδιανοί, καὶ Σατορνιλιανοί· ἕκαστος ἰδίως καὶ ἑτέρως ἰδίαν δόξαν παρεισηγάγησαν· ἀπὸ τούτων ψευδόχριστοι· ψευδοπροφῆται· ψευδαπόστολοι.

(*H. E.* IV. 22.)

That is, according to Hegesippus, the first trouble in the Church at Jerusalem arose from the ambition of Thebuthis: Thebuthis wanted to be the head of the Church in Jerusalem, at a time when it was a Judaeo-Christian Church; he was himself sprung from one or other of the seven great Jewish sects. It was not merely the case that a single ambitious person from this quarter upset the unity of the Church. All the great heresies sprang from the same root: to wit, the Simonians from Simon Magus, the Dositheans from Dositheus, the Gortheonians from Gorthaeus, the Masbothaeans from Masbotheos. And from these again sprang the heresies named after Menander, Marcion, Carpocrates, Valentinus, Basilides, Satornilus, and all the rest of the anti-Christian brood.

There can be no doubt that we have here the same statement that we found in our verses on Matthew the Monk. We are dealing with very early matter.

It is not necessary to hold up the argument unduly over the objection that Marcion and Marcionism can hardly be described as a heresy having its roots in Judaism; it has not unnaturally been suggested that for Marcion we might read Marcus the Gnostic. I do not propose to change the text because, paradoxical as it may seem, it is not inconsistent with reality that an anti-Judaic heresy should have its roots in a foundation, which itself may be regarded as Jewish. As Harnack points out:

The bold anti-judaist was the disciple of a Jewish thinker, Paul, and the origin of Marcion's antinomianism may be ultimately found in the prophets.

It is, then, quite possible that some early Christians did not go so far as to reach to Paul in their explanation of the origin of Marcionism, but attributed it to some intermediate, or even hostile, Jewish development. Leaving this question on one side, for it is not vital for our present inquiry, let us return to Hegesippus and his story of the seven Jewish sects.

At this point, we have to draw attention to a curious piece of evidence that may lead us to interesting and unexpected conclusions.

In the work of Bar Ṣalibi against the Jews, which we easily see to be almost entirely composed of early Testimonies, we find that, instead of plunging at once, as Cyprian does, into extracts from the Old Testament, he treats us to a preface concerning the various sects among the Jews: first of all making some remarks to the effect that the Jews have relapsed into idolatry, stoned the prophets and crucified the Beloved Son; and then, in the next place, explaining to us the origin of the Jewish name in the patriarch Judah, to whose tribe the kingdom belonged, from whom it came as a title of great honour to the people who are named after him. Then he says:

> But it is time for us to tell of the divisions which arose among them, the heresies of the house of the Jews.

So he begins to enumerate and to describe successively the Scribes, Pharisees, Sadducees, Hemerobaptists, Essenes, Osseans, Nazaraeans, Herodians. Here are eight primal Jewish heresies, which may be compared with the seven of Hegesippus. The statement of Hegesippus is as follows:

> There were various opinions current among the men of the circumcision, the children of Israel, on the part of those who were *in opposition to the tribe of Judah and the Messiah*: to wit: Essenes, Galileans, Hemerobaptists, Masbotheans, Samaritans, Sadducees, Pharisees.

The coincidences between Bar Ṣalibi and Hegesippus are not confined to the recurrence of a number of names, and an almost exact numerical equivalence; there is the further agreement in the allusion to the tribe of Judah which precedes: it cannot be accidental that Hegesippus should speak in such friendly terms of the tribe of Judah as almost to make one think that that tribe was outside the circle of heresy, and that Bar Ṣalibi should have a special section to explain the Judaean name and its excellence as coming from Judah the Praising One. There seems to be some underlying connexion between the two writers. The antiquity of Bar Ṣalibi's list may be seen from the fact of its almost exact agreement with the catalogue of Epiphanius, which runs as follows: "Scribes, Pharisees, Sadducees, Essenes, Nazoreans, Hemerobaptists, Herodians."

All that I want to establish at this point (without going after other heretical lists) is that there was a catalogue of seven Jewish heresies, probably coupled with some commendatory remarks on the tribe of Judah and perhaps earlier than the time of Hegesippus.

Now turn to Justin's *Dialogue with Trypho* c. 80, and we shall find him working off a list of seven Jewish heresies, though it does not agree in detail with the list of Hegesippus. He says that people who do not believe in the resurrection of the body are not to be called Christians, any more than we should give the name of Jews to Sadducees, or similar heretics, such as the Genistae and Meristae, the Galileans, the Hellenians, the Pharisees and the Baptists. It was a curious thing to say that Jewish heretics are not to be counted Jews, but it coincides with what we have noted in Hegesippus and Bar Ṣalibi. Justin does not need to explain to Trypho philologically the meaning of the term *Judaeus*; but in his *Apology* to the Roman senate he is careful to explain the origin of *Judaeus* in the tribe of Judah.

The conclusion to which we are being led is that there is some common matter that is attracting the attention of these three writers; in the case of Bar Ṣalibi we are definitely dealing with a *Book of Testimonies*: in the case of Justin the *Book of Testimonies* certainly underlies the *Apology* and the *Dialogue with Trypho*.

It remains, then, to be seen whether the *Book of Testimonies* which we have shown to become, from a mere polemic, the foundation of a book of Christian doctrine, was also in the hands of Hegesippus.

The common opinion about Hegesippus is that he is an ecclesiastical historian, the first member of that family. The opinion is based upon the fact that we receive from him the story of the martyrdom of St James the Just, the account of the arrest of certain members of our Lord's family by Domitian, etc.

It is, however, possible that the title of ecclesiastical historian is not the correct one by which to describe him, any more than we should give the title to Papias, because he tells us details of the death of Judas, and of the relations between Mark and Peter.

Eusebius' account of Hegesippus' work is as follows:

ἐν πέντε δὲ οὖν συγγράμμασιν οὗτος τὴν ἀπλανῆ παράδοσιν τοῦ Ἀποστολικοῦ κηρύγματος ἁπλουστάτῃ, συντάξει γραφῆς ὑπομνηματισάμενος.

(Euseb. *H. E.* IV. 8.)

i.e. Hegesippus wrote five books on the Apostolical Preaching with
a very full literary illustration (lit. making his memorials with a
very full composition of writing). Now here we are struck by
two things. One is the title *Apostolical Preaching,* which we have
already had in the newly found work of Irenaeus (a work which
we have shown to be saturated with matter taken over from the
Testimony Book), and the other is that the work is divided into
five books, precisely as Papias' work on the *Dominical Oracles* was,
a work which we showed ground for suspecting to be a commentary
on the *Testimony Book* which must have been, on that showing,
itself divided into five sections.

The coincidences are so remarkable that we are led to the
suggestion that Hegesippus is doing the same thing as Papias;
he is commenting on the *Prophetical Testimonies* and finding
illustrations and expansions for the doctrines there involved or
laid down. Hegesippus' description of the tradition of the *Apostolical Preaching* as ἀπλανής ("free from error"), if the word
really goes back to Hegesippus himself, may very well be due to
a contrast with the πλανὴ Ἰουδαική such as we find described in
the verses which we were discussing.

Now let us test our hypothesis and see whether it illuminates
the field of study. If Hegesippus is really one of the train of
commentators on a book of Old Testament extracts, we ought to
find verifications of this supposed dependence in the fragments of
Hegesippus which have been preserved for us by Eusebius. Of
these, the principal one is the story of the martyrdom of St James
the Just. We are told that some persons of the seven heresies,
which Hegesippus had already described, tried to persuade St
James to allay the chiliastic expectations of the crowds who had
come to the Passover, and who were evidently on the *qui vive*
with regard to an immediate second coming of Jesus. St James
refuses to be persuaded, and adds his testimony to the general
expectation; whereupon he is thrown down from the temple
battlements into the ravine of the Kedron, and what life was left
in him was beaten out with a fuller's club.

There are some curious points in the narrative: first of all it
is said that St James was known by the titles of "The Just," and
"The Bulwark of the People," and it is significantly added that
"the prophets themselves bear witness on this point." Why the
prophets should concern themselves with St James the Just or

his martyrdom can only be explained by our finding the Just man in the Old Testament and by our finding him ill-treated.

In the next place, we are told that when the Scribes and Pharisees (or whatever heretics they were) decided on putting the Just man to death, they fulfilled the word written in Isaiah:

> Let us away with (ἄρωμεν) the Just man, for he is displeasing to us; therefore they shall eat the fruits of their works.

So it is not unnatural to conjecture that St James was identified with the Just man of Isaiah iii. 10, and that this prophecy was taken to represent his treatment at the hands of the Jews.

We may easily satisfy ourselves that this passage is amongst the earliest of the *Testimonies against the Jews*. It occurs, for example, in Cyp. *Test.* III. 14 in the form

> *Quod ipse sit justus, quem Judaei occisuri essent.* In Sapientia Solomonis: Circumveniamus justum quoniam insuavis est nobis et contrarius est operibus nostris, etc. (*Sap. Sol.* II. 12–17, 19–22),

for which the corresponding Greek of the Septuagint is

> ἐνεδρεύσωμεν τὸν δίκαιον, ὅτι δύσχρηστος ἡμῖν ἐστιν, καὶ ἐναντιοῦται τοῖς ἔργοις ἡμῶν.

We notice that the author of the *Wisdom of Solomon* has been quoting Isaiah, only substituting ἐνεδρεύσομεν for δήσωμεν of the LXX. The Testimony might, apparently, come from either writer, but Hegesippus, who says ἄρωμεν, makes the connexion with Isaiah, and Cyprian makes his reference (correctly enough) to the *Wisdom of Solomon*.

Then there is this further difference that while Cyprian refers the prophetic quotation to Jesus, Hegesippus says the Just One is James.

It will be worth our while to look a little closer into the quotation as it occurs in the earliest writers. Barnabas (c. 6) quotes the verse from Isaiah of Christ's sufferings (reading δήσωμεν) and says the prophet spoke it ἐπὶ τὸν Ἰσραήλ. Evidently he had it so in his book of extracts.

Justin, who, by the way, appears to avoid reference to the Wisdom books (with the exception of Proverbs which he calls Sophia), quotes the passage from Isaiah (with ἄρωμεν and a variant δήσωμεν), and says that the Jews have gone to such a pitch of wickedness as to hate the Just One whom they murdered, and those who had from him received (the grace) to be what they are, pious, *just* and lovers of their kind. Here the Jews are said to hate the Just man and his Just men. We become suspicious of a double reference.

In Bar Ṣalibi the reference is made to *Sap. Sol.* as follows:

And Solomon says (speaking in the person of the Jews): Let us destroy the righteous because he is unpleasing to us; for he opposes, etc.

Lactantius (IV. 16) follows the text of Cyprian almost exactly.

It seems, then, that there are two traditions, of which the earliest appears to be the reference to Isaiah, which may have been expanded later by reference to *Sap. Sol.*: there is, however, the possibility that both passages may have occurred in the early collections, for it is clear from Cyprian that, if there is one section in which the Jews are said to have slain the Just Christ, there was another (I. 2) in which they are said to have slain the prophets.

There is nothing, then, impossible in the supposition that Hegesippus may have charged the Jews with murder under both heads. He has certainly included St James among the victims of Isaiah iii. 10: and he has recorded the incident of his death as a fulfilment of prophecy, in language that we find current in the *Testimony Books.* We may, therefore, add this fact to our previous observation of Hegesippus' derivation of the seven sects of Judaism from the *Testimonia adversus Judaeos.*

We have, perhaps, said enough to establish Hegesippus' acquaintance with the anti-Judaic collections, but not enough to deprive him of his right to the title of ecclesiastical historian. In that case, we ought not to lay further stress on his writing in five volumes, until we can co-ordinate what we know of his writings more closely with the known sequence of the anti-Judaic arguments. He has certainly helped us to elucidate a number of obscure points, and especially to put Matthew the Monk on a right footing.

Before leaving this discussion it may be well to remark that it is quite practicable to use a *Testimony Book*, not only as the pattern of apostolical preaching, but also as a series of pegs upon which to hang historical observations. When, for example, we learn from Papias non-canonical details as to the death of Judas, the motive for introducing them may very well be the fact that Judas and the fate of Judas occupy an important place in the supposed verification of prophecy. We have seen this indirectly in the twenty-seventh chapter of Matthew, and its reference to

Jeremy the prophet. We need not doubt that the action of Judas was recorded in the first draft of the *Testimony Book*, the action, I say, and not the fate: for if there had been anything corresponding to the hanging of Judas, Papias could not have embellished the tradition with his story of the bursting asunder of the bad man, under the pressure of a passing carriage. There was ground before Papias upon which he could build; and no doubt similar cases might be discovered.

The net result of this part of the inquiry appears to be that there was

(*a*) a primitive book of prophetical quotations:

(*b*) that these were divided into five sections:

(*c*) which five sections became the basis of Papias' commentary in five consequent books;

and (*d*) perhaps of the five books of Hegesippus on the Apostolical Preaching:

(*e*) this primitive book in five sections was attributed to Matthew;

and (*f*) survives in such a five-fold division in the work described as *Matthew the Monk against the Jews*.

It remains to be determined whether this primitive collection was first extant in Aramaic, or whether this is only an ill-considered guess of Papias, which later writers have made worse by assuming that he spoke of the *Gospel* of Matthew of which we are certain that no Aramaic origin can directly be affirmed.

CHAPTER XIII

A FURTHER PROOF OF THE MATTHAEAN ORIGIN OF THE *BOOK OF TESTIMONIES*

In the previous chapter we were able to show that the *Book of Testimonies against the Jews* continued to be transcribed in a modified form of the original Greek as late as, or later than, the invention of printing; and that in the latest form which we were able to trace, it still bore the name of Matthew, and contained reminiscences of an original division into five sections: from which we inferred that the original *Dominical Oracles*, upon which Papias wrote five books of Commentary in the early part of the second century, were precisely the same thing as an early collection of proof-texts of Christian doctrine from the Old Testament, attributed to Matthew, which lies behind the anti-Judaic writings of Cyprian, Gregory of Nyssa, and other patristic writers. We now propose to confirm these inferences by reference to a curious passage contained in a fragment of Victorinus of Pettau.

Victorinus is a writer whose *floruit* is somewhere about the year 300 A.D. (for he was martyred in the Diocletian persecution) but whose critical value is far higher than his age. He is only known to us from a few stray fragments and references (the latter of which are mainly due to Jerome or to the satellites of Jerome). His value lies in the fact that he was the most unblushing of the patristic plagiarists, and that he was in the habit of transcribing his favourite authors with the minimum of modification, or of literally translating them from Greek into not very polished Latin, and re-issuing his transcriptions and translations under his own name. For this reason he is to be held in the highest esteem by all students of Christian antiquity, whose one regret when they recognize Victorinus' literary method, is that we have nothing left of his work except a Commentary upon the Apocalypse and a few trivial (or apparently trivial) fragments. If he only had written more when it was so easy for him to write! And if more of what he had written had been preserved! The wish is the more poignant when we observe, on the one hand, with Jerome, that he transcribes Origen, and when we find out, on the other hand, that he treated Papias in the same way that he had operated upon Origen. For Jerome expressly tells us that Victorinus treated Origen, not as an interpreter, but as if he were the very author of his works: and it is not difficult to infer from an examination of the portions of Victorinus' commentary on the Apocalypse which have come to light that he treated Papias in the very same manner. On this point I wrote something in the *Expositor* for 1895 (pp. 448 sqq.) under the heading of *A New Patristic Fragment*. The article was suggested by the announcement in the *Theologisches Literaturblatt* for April 26th of that year, of the discovery by Professor Haussleiter, of Greifswald, of the commentary of Victorinus on the Apocalypse in a new MS. in the Vatican (Cod. Ottobonianus latinus 3288A). From the text of the MS. my friend Haussleiter came to the conclusion that we were face to face with earlier material that had been borrowed either from Papias or from the Elders of whom Irenaeus speaks. At this point I am not anxious to repeat or expand the arguments for the servile dependence of Victorinus upon Papias. Such dependence was admitted by Jerome in the case of Victorinus' translations of Origen, and might almost have been inferred in the case of Papias from other references of Jerome to the chiliasm of Victorinus and its connexion with the similar chiliasm of Papias. We will, however, give one playful illustration of the art of transfer as practised by Victorinus which may escape the notice of the critic who is not studying carefully the dependence of one writer upon another.

It is well known that Eusebius speaks of Papias as a person who was

$$\pi \acute{a} \nu \upsilon \ \sigma \mu \iota \kappa \rho \grave{o} \varsigma \ \tau \grave{o} \nu \ \nu o \widehat{\upsilon} \nu$$

and this description of Papias as a person of quite inferior intelligence was contradicted (apparently) by another passage in which he is described by Eusebius as ἀνὴρ λογιώτατος. It was difficult to believe that Eusebius, who was himself a very learned person, could have imagined that great learning and great stupidity could be characteristics of the same person. Such cases might occur, alas! they do sometimes occur; but Eusebius was not the man to point them out. It was not an unnatural suggestion, then, which was made to me by my friend Dom Chapman, that Eusebius was quoting Papias' modest estimate of his own powers[1], when he said he was stupid, and giving his own judgment of Papias' ability when he said he was a very learned person. The modesty of Papias in judging himself and the charity of Eusebius in estimating him do not involve any contradiction.

Now if we turn to Victorinus in the fragment which has been preserved of his work on the *Creation of the World* we find him beginning a section as follows:

Nunc ergo de innarrabili gloria Dei et providentia videas memorari; tamen, *ut mens parva poterit,* conabor ostendere. (Routh, *Rell.* 3. 460.)

Here we have the very same affectation of modesty as in Papias; and since the *mens parva* of Victorinus answers exactly to νοῦς σμικρός, we infer that Victorinus is copying Papias literally, and translating him verbally, even to the extent of appropriating Papias' personal depreciation of his own abilities. The illustration will serve to show the kind of dependence exhibited by a writer who transcribes another and appropriates to himself what he transcribes.

Enough has been said by way of reminder as to the literary method employed by Victorinus of Pettau. Now let us turn to a curious passage in his discussion of the Sabbath, which he wishes to interpret in a millenarian manner; the true Sabbath being the thousand years when the saints shall reign with Christ. He tells us then:

Et apud Matthaeum scriptum legimus; Esaias quoque et caeteri collegae ejus Sabbatum resolverunt; ut verum illud et justum sabbatum septimo milliario annorum observaretur. (Routh, *Rell.* 3. 458.)

The passage has caused great perplexity: for where do we find any reference in the Gospel of Matthew to the evacuation of the Sabbath by *Isaiah* and his colleagues? Routh suggests that Isaiah is a mistake for *David,* and that the reference is to Matthew xii. 3, where Jesus asks the Pharisees whether they have never read what *David* did when he was hungry and when he and those who were with him (his colleagues, if we so interpret Victorinus) ate the tabooed shew-bread. There are objections, however, to the removal of Isaiah in this way from the text.

In the first place, we remember the opening verses of Isaiah, in which the Lord says that he hates the new moons and sabbaths

---

[1] *H. E.* III. 39: Σφόδρα γάρ τοι σμικρὸς ὢν τὸν νοῦν, ὡς ἂν ἐκ τῶν αὐτοῦ λόγων τεκμηράμενον εἰπεῖν, φαίνεται.

of the Jews: the first chapter of Isaiah is constantly in quotation by the anti-Judaic writers; there is no reason therefore why Isaiah should not have stood in the text. In the next place, Victorinus is certainly working from conventional Testimonies: a few lines back he quotes the breach of the Sabbath by Joshua at the siege of Jericho, as follows:

Jesus quoque Naue, successor Moysis, et ipse sabbatum resolvit, die enim Sabbati praecipit filiis Israel ut muros civitatis Hiericho tubicinibus circuirent, et bellum allophylis indicarent.

We say that this is conventional anti-Judaic Testimony: if we look in Gregory of Nyssa's section on the Sabbath, we shall find the following sentence:

ἐπεί τοι τίνος ἕνεκεν ὁ Ἰησοῦς ὁ τοῦ Ναυῆ κυκλῶν τὴν Ἰεριχὼ μετὰ σαλπίγγων ἐπὶ ἑπτὰ ἡμέρας, οὐκ ἐσχόλασε τῷ σαββάτῳ;

We may find the same anti-Judaic argument drawn from the military operations around Jericho in other early writers. For instance, in Tertullian *adv. Judaeos* c. 4, we shall find the same reference to the breach of the Sabbath at Jericho, followed, as in Victorinus, by a reference to the Sabbath-breaking of the Maccabees. It is more to our purpose to quote Gregory of Nyssa, because it proves definitely that the argument involved belongs to a *book* of anti-Judaic quotations, which might not be so certainly conceded in other writers who make the same references.

Victorinus, then, has the *Book of Testimonies* before him: and there was an anti-Sabbatic section in the book. We note in passing that the section has disappeared from Cyprian, and is not very strongly represented in Gregory of Nyssa. For our purpose it is sufficient to show that it existed in the source of Victorinus.

We come next to the supposed quotation from Isaiah by way of Matthew: and we say that we have a right to expect at this point that anti-Sabbatic language of Isaiah which we referred just now to Tertullian *adv. Judaeos*. The third chapter of this treatise is occupied with the proof that the ancient circumcision and the prior law are done away. Then in the fourth chapter we come to the question of the Sabbath. The argument is as follows: the abolition of the ancient law involves the suspension of the observance of the Sabbath. The Jews throw at us a precept of the decalogue: we infer from that same precept that we ought to abstain from servile work on every day of the week and so keep a perpetual Sabbath: but we may also point out that there are two Sabbaths to be kept, one the temporal Sabbath, the other the eternal Sabbath; and against the Jews' mode of sabbatizing,

> *Dicit Esaias propheta*: Sabbata vestra odit anima mea.

The text of Victorinus, accordingly, must not be altered from Isaiah to David: and the natural explanation of the curious reference to Matthew for a passage in Isaiah would seem to be that the *Testimony Book* was attributed to Matthew in the sources of Victorinus, *i.e.* as we have seen, in the commentaries of Papias.

We may confirm our conclusion in another way: the text of Victorinus is extremely faulty and difficult to edit; but we do not alter either *Isaiah* or *Matthew*. The curious expression

> Esaias et caeteri collegae ejus

requires some consideration: it might perhaps be taken to mean

> Isaiah and the rest of the prophets who deal with the subject of the Sabbath;

it seems, however, to be probable that *caeteri collegae ejus* should be corrected to

> *caeterae eclogae ejus ;*

in which case the words refer to Matthew and not to Isaiah and the title of Matthew's book will be

> *Select Testimonies ;*

for the heading of the work of Gregory of Nyssa to which we have been referring is precisely

> ἐκλογαὶ μαρτυριῶν πρὸς Ἰουδαίους.

Unless, then, we are very much astray in our treatment of the subject, we have established that Papias (and following him Victorinus) used a book of ἐκλογαὶ μαρτυριῶν compiled by Matthew the Apostle[1]. We have thus confirmed the conclusions at which we arrived by a study of the MS. at the Monastery of the Iberians on Mount Athos.

Before we leave this part of the inquiry we may ask whether the Victorinus (Papias) fragment has anything more to say on the subject of the *Testimonies*.

---

[1] The same use of ἐκλογαί to describe a book of Old Testament extracts is involved in Eusebius' extract from the dedicatory section of Melito to his disciple Onesimus, who had asked him to make ἐκλογὰς ἔκ τε τοῦ νόμου καὶ τῶν προφητῶν περὶ τοῦ Σωτῆρος καὶ πάσης τῆς πίστεως ἡμῶν.

Victorinus concludes his argument for the millennial Sabbath, on the ground that the world will last 6000 years, and that a thousand years are as a day with God. So we get six days and then the seventh. He then dilates on the sanctity of the Heptad, showing that there are seven heavens and seven spirits of God, seven heavens made by Christ and seven spirits descending upon Christ: his proof-texts are as follows:

Verbo Domini coeli firmati sunt et spiritu oris ejus omnis virtus eorum.

This is Ps. xxxii. 6, and will be found in Cyp. *Test.* II. 3.

Et requiescet super eum spiritus sapientiae, et intellectus, spiritus consilii, et virtutis, spiritus scientiae, et pietatis, et inplevit illum spiritus timoris Dei.

This is Is. xi. 2, 3, and will be found in Cyp. *Test.* II. 11.

The next passage is our old friend, with a slight modification;

Eructatum est cor meum verbum bonum;

which is Ps. xlv. 1, and Cyp. *Test.* II. 3; and it is followed as in Cyprian by the opening verses of the Prologue of St John's Gospel.

It is clear that the arithmetical by-play of Victorinus centres in the *Book of Testimonies,* and some, at least, of his curious numerical associations go back to Papias, along with his chiliasm.

The importance of these investigations must be admitted. They take us back to what we may now call the Matthew Book of the early Church, and to the first manifesto of Christian doctrine contained therein.

As to the Victorinus fragment we hope to have more to say at no very distant date.

CHAPTER XIV

PROFESSOR BURKITT AND THE *TESTIMONIA*

The foregoing results have brought us to a complete verification of the thesis that the original *Testimonia* of the Christian Church were collected by Matthew the Apostle, and circulated in the first instance under his name; they are the *Logia* to which Papias refers, and these Logia are not the *Sayings of Jesus*, as one was at first inclined to assume. The two collections, the *Sayings of Jesus* and the *Testimonia*, are of similar antiquity, and, as I have frequently pointed out, antedate the literature of the New Testament.

At this point, my results will be found to coincide with Professor Burkitt's, but with this exception, that he made the right identification of the Logia, where I made, at first, the incorrect selection, which I have now rectified. It is a good point at which to compare results, and it will give confidence to students who compare our diverse methods and independent investigations, and observe the coincidence, more or less definite, of our results.

Prof. Burkitt's questions will be found elaborated in his book *The Gospel History and its Transmission*: by working on the O.T. quotations in the Gospel of Matthew, he came to the conclusion that those quotations were not capable of reference to either the Septuagint or the Hebrew text: sometimes the Hebrew text, or a variation of it, is in evidence, and sometimes it is the LXX. Upon which Prof. Burkitt remarks[1]:

The Evangelist was after all not unfamiliar with the Greek Bible. This is not surprising: the surprising part is the influence of the Hebrew text in a Greek Gospel. Now, as we have seen, the evidence does not point to the direct use of a Hebrew MS. of the Old Testament: we must look rather to a collection of *Testimonia* as the immediate source of our Evangelist's quotations. The collection must have been made from the Hebrew, but the names of the several prophets or psalmists do not seem to have been attached to

[1] p. 126.

the quotations, nor were the words always cited with scrupulous accuracy. To correct and apply the oracles of the Old Testament in the light of the New Dispensation was the first literary task of the Christian Church. Several such collections survive, and one of them, the *Testimonia* edited by Cyprian, is the source upon which a whole series of Latin writers quote Scripture.

So far, Prof. Burkitt's argument for the existence of a lost *Testimony Book* appears to be confirmed by our inquiry, but with some hesitation as to details. For example, there is not the slightest support for Burkitt's theory that the *Testimonia* were issued without the names of authors. There is no trace of any unauthorized testifying: everywhere we find names given and names misunderstood and confused with one another; and indeed, the *Testimonia* would have been greatly reduced in value, if there were no indications of the persons who give the Testimony.

Then, I think, there should have been some hesitation as to the immediate Hebrew ancestry of the *Testimonies*. All O.T. quotations are, of course, ultimately Hebrew (omitting certain Apocryphal books). It does not, however, follow that the Hebrew dialect which Papias assigns to the Matthew book was what we call classical Hebrew: it may have just as well been Aramaic. We need some further study of the origin of the collection before we can speak so certainly. Prof. Burkitt follows up his conjecture as to the existence of a *Testimony Book* by the further speculation, to which we alluded above, that the *Testimony Book* is the *Matthew-Book*. His exact language is as follows:

We may go on to conjecture that the original collection of Messianic proof-texts was made by Matthew the Publican in Hebrew, and that it is the use of this document by our Evangelist which gives his work the right to be called the Gospel according to Matthew. This collection of texts, in a word, may have been the famous Λόγια, of which Papias speaks (Euseb. *H. E.* III. 39), which each one interpreted as he could. The chief objection to this view is that such a quotation as that in Matt. ii. 15 ("Out of Egypt have I called my son") seems to assume the story of the flight into Egypt, and it is difficult to believe that this story had a place in the work of the Apostle Matthew. I do not think we are in a position to solve the difficulty. The *Logia* of S. Matthew is hopelessly lost, and we do not know what it really contained.

The language is a trifle too pessimistic, but then pioneers always cultivate a pessimistic strain. For instance, Frazer, who has solved so many odd riddles of the universe, wrote me recently to say that he did not believe the Greek mythology would ever be resolved! I was busily engaged on Olympus at the time!

It is surely not correct to say that the *Logia* of Matthew is hopelessly lost and its contents indeterminable, when we have a late form of the book preserved on Mt Athos, and when we can, by internal criticism of the earliest Fathers, restore whole blocks of it. Prof. Burkitt was confining himself in his investigation too closely to the O.T. quotations in Matthew. It does not seem necessary to assume that all these quotations are actually taken from the Logia book. We can work the matter out, if need be, without consulting the Gospel of Matthew at all. If, however, it is necessary to regard the proof-text in Matthew ii. 15 as taken from the *Testimonia* this would not involve us in a belief in the Apostolic authorship of the flight into Egypt. The proof-text may have been misunderstood by the historian, whoever it was, that wrote down the incident. It is possible that what was proved in the first case by the quotation was that Christ was called Israel, for which a sufficient demonstration was found in the words,

> When *Israel* was a child I loved him;
> And out of Egypt I called my *son*.

A person hunting for identifications might very well equate the Son with Israel, on the faith of just such a passage, that is to say, if he really wanted to prove from the Scriptures that Christ was Israel. Now it admits of demonstration that some early Christian writers did want to make such an equation. We recall, for instance, how Justin Martyr in his *Dialogue with Trypho* occupies himself over and over, with the thesis that Christ is Israel. It will be interesting to examine some of his proofs and to connect them with the *Book of Testimonies*. If this can be done there will at least be a possibility, as I have said, that the original use of the passage about the calling of the Son out of Egypt may have been to prove this very point that Christ is the Israel of the Old Testament. Even if I do not succeed in proving that something like this was in the original Matthew book, I should still lament Prof. Burkitt's pessimistic statements as to its contents and possible recovery: while at the same time, I think I have proved that in his identification of the Logia book, his intuition was more correct and his vision wider than my own.

What, then, of the problem that has emerged of the possible identification of Christ with Israel? We are to examine Justin Martyr's language on the point, reminding ourselves at the

beginning of the inquiry of the way in which the Cyprianic
Testimonies show the building up of successive proofs that

	Christ is Sophia;
that	Christ is the Logos;
that	Christ is the Hand of God;
that	Christ is the Lord and God;
that	Christ is the Stone, etc. etc.

Is it possible that there was once a section that
Christ is Israel and Jacob?

In *Dial.* 36, we find Justin explaining to Trypho, that he wants
to follow a set order in the prophecies which he proposes to quote;
and if you will allow me, he says, I will prove to you that "Christ
is God and Lord of Hosts, and that he is symbolically called Jacob
by the Holy Spirit." We notice that the first half of the Justin-
thesis is a Testimony heading. Probably, then, the same thing
is true of the second half.

In *Dial.* 75, Justin plays with the equivalence of the name
Jesus and that of Joshua, of whom Moses is informed "that my
name is in my angel." God will send His angel before His people:
the name of the angel is Jesus. Thus we have a proof of the
Testimony heading, that Christ is called Ἄγγελος. Justin then
continues:

> Yes, and he is also called Israel, and the name of Jacob was changed into
> that very name.

Thus Christ is called Israel and Jacob.

In *Dial.* 100, Justin remarks, "I have already demonstrated
to you that *Christ is called Jacob and Israel....* In the books of
the prophets he is addressed as the Wisdom and the Day and the
Dawn (or Branch) and the Sword and the Rod and *Jacob and
Israel.*" Here Justin starts with the first chapter of the Cyprianic
Christology, that Christ is the Wisdom of God, and goes on to
prove that Christ is Israel. With this we should compare
Dial. 126.

"Who is this, who is sometimes called Angel of the Great
Counsel, and by Ezekiel a man, and by Daniel one like the son of
man, and by Isaiah a child, and by David is called Christ and
Θεὸς προσκυνητός, and by many others is called Christ and a
Stone, and is called Sophia by Solomon, and by Moses is called
Joseph and Judah and a star, and by Zachariah is called the

Dawn (or Branch) and again by Isaiah is called the Suffering One, and *Jacob and Israel,* and Rod and Flower and Corner-Stone, and Son of God."

Nearly all of this comes out of the *Testimonia,* and we infer that in the same source there was a section which proved that Christ was the Israel of the Old Testament.

We give this as a specimen of the method in which such writings as those of Justin may be employed in the restoration of the missing fragments of the Logia or Matthew-Book.

CHAPTER XV

AN ANONYMOUS WRITER ON THE ORACLES OF PAPIAS

In the previous chapter I have drawn attention to the relation between the results arrived at in the present volume, and those which are adumbrated by Prof. Burkitt in his work on *The Gospel History and its Transmission.* The work in question was published in 1906. It was reviewed by v. Dobschütz in the *Theol. Lit. Zeitung* for August 17th, 1907, without the slightest reference to the statements which Burkitt makes as to the existence of an "original collection of Messianic proof-texts made by Matthew the Publican in Hebrew" and the equation of this collection with "the famous Λόγια of which Papias speaks, which each one interpreted as he could." It is curious that the most far-reaching of all the statements and conjectures in Prof. Burkitt's volume of published lectures should have escaped notice in this way at the hands of an expert!

I am now going to show that another and a somewhat earlier writer has made similar statements, and been the subject of an even more pronounced neglect.

In the year 1894 appeared an anonymous work entitled *The Oracles ascribed to Matthew by Papias of Hierapolis*[1], whose thesis as declared in the Preface was as follows:

That the famous work, λόγων κυριακῶν ἐξήγησις by Papias of Hierapolis, was upon the interpretation of Messianic prophecies, and that the work referred to in it, and attributed to Matthew, consisted of a collection of Messianic prophecies in Hebrew, extracted from the Old Testament, and perhaps from other books.

It will be noted at once that the writer is working upon the same lines as Prof. Burkitt and myself, and his date shows that he is working independently, if evidence were necessary on that point, which of course it is not, for the investigation which follows is first-hand work and of great importance. Like Prof. Burkitt, he prefixes the word "Messianic" to his supposed prophecies, and

---

[1] Published by Longmans, Green & Co.

keeps to the language of Papias in affirming them to have been
written in Hebrew. As we have shown that the *Testimony Book*
which we all three discover is really the original book of Christian
doctrine, and that the prophecies are not exclusively Messianic,
it would, perhaps, have been better not to prefix the adjective in
question, and to have kept to a wider view of the Old Testament
prophecies, such as Cyprian's *Testimonia* would have suggested to
us; and it would also have been wiser to keep more clearly in
view the ambiguity of such a term as "the Hebrew dialect."
Setting aside these preliminary criticisms upon the language of
the Preface (they will be repeated instinctively throughout the
book, as we read it), let us see how the anonymous writer goes to
work in the unfolding of his thesis.

His chief argument is that the word *Logia* properly belongs to
extracts from the Old Testament:

> The Fathers quoted the Old Testament from secondary sources, that is
> to say, that collections of texts upon particular topics were made either by
> the persons making the quotations or other authors, and that such collections
> were the immediate source of the quotations[1].

It is evident that if such collections can be demonstrated to have
existed, and if it can also be shown that the term *Logia* properly
belongs to O.T. extracts, then the inference will be easy that the
Logia of Papias were a collection of Old Testament prophecies.
Accordingly, the writer devotes himself to this latter point. He
says:

> I carefully studied Dr Lightfoot's essay in the *Contemporary Review.*
> I here saw that in all the instances given by him, that were before or not long
> after the time of Papias, the word λόγια was applied to the Old Testament[2].

I have expressed in the previous pages the opinion that it is
not possible to make such a sharp distinction between λόγια and
λόγοι as is commonly made. This does not prevent us from
agreeing that there are a sufficient number of cases in which λόγια
does express Oracles from the Old Testament; and if that be
conceded, the next step can readily be taken, namely, the
suggestion that it is probable that Papias' *Oracles* (or *Dominical
Oracles*) are a collection of Old Testament extracts. The chief
difficulty will lie, not with the Oracles, but with the title Dominical
that is prefixed to them. It may be asked why Old Testament
prophecies should have this label attached to them.

[1] Preface, p. vi. n.   [2] Preface, p. viii.

Our writer re-states his case as follows:

I submit, therefore, there can be no doubt that by the word λόγια Papias should be taken to intend the Old Testament Scriptures, if that interpretation will satisfy the context. Taking this, then, to be so, the title of the work of Papias will be, "An exposition of Old Testament Scriptures relating to the Lord, that is of Messianic prophecies[1]."

And he confirms his explanation of the *Dominical Oracles* by reference to the work of Melito, which he described as *Selections* (ἐκλογαί) *from the Law and the Prophets about the Saviour, and our whole faith,* where the language, indeed, shows that the prophecies related to the Saviour, but then it must also be included that they applied to the whole range of the Christian faith, and not merely to the Messianic aspect of it. It may be noted, in passing, that after proving, or at least going a long way to prove, that the Oracles came from the Old Testament, the writer includes the Apocalypse of John amongst the books from which selection was made: he says:

Papias' work consisted of comments upon the Old Testament and perhaps also on some part of the Apocalypse, *which he may have regarded as equivalent to one of the prophets[2].*

This is with the view of explaining how the millenarian elements could have been introduced into Papias' discourses: it might also be argued from the same point of view that Papias' *Logia* might also have contained matter from the Gospels. It would have been better to base the millenarian parts of the text of Papias on the Old Testament, and to have referred the coincidences with the Apocalypse to the commentary.

The writer concludes this part of the argument with the statement:

By the word λόγια or oracles, Papias meant the Old Testament, or some part of it, and when Papias says that Matthew wrote or compiled the oracles he means that he wrote a catena of Old Testament prophecies[3].

This is the first part of the argument of the book: in the next part the writer goes on to discuss the Messianic prophecies which occur in the Gospels and in early writers such as Justin Martyr and Irenaeus, with the object of showing the existence of a common source behind them. In the course of the argument he lights on the very passages with which we commenced our own study of the matter; and thus presents the argument of the present volume in the inverse order. He sees, for instance, that the printed text of

---

[1] *Oracles,* 82.   [2] *Ibid.* 128.   [3] *Ibid.* 128.

Irenaeus is wrong in reading *Balaam* for *Isaiah* in the famous Star-passage. He does not see how Isaiah came to be in the text; but he says very correctly,

There can be no doubt that the reading of the Vossian codex exhibits the true text of Irenaeus. No reason can be supposed why any transcriber of Irenaeus who found Balaam, should erroneously substitute Isaiah, and at the same time stumble into agreement with Justin in such an obvious blunder......We are driven to the conclusion that Irenaeus quoted from some source other than the LXX, from which Justin also quoted[1].

Thus the anonymous writer ends up where we began our investigation, and where we are tempted to say that he ought also to have commenced; for the existence of the *Testimony Book* does not depend upon the interpretation of a passage or two in a single writer like Papias. It lies in evidence everywhere, and ought to be sought for over a wider area than those passages which refer to the *Logia*. Setting this criticism on one side (for after all the result is the important thing and not the choice of methods by which the result is to be reached), we have pointed out that the argument of the anonymous writer to whom we have been referring is a just one, and that his results coincide, for the most part, with those reached in the present volume. It is quite possible that there may be other writers to whose intuitions or arguments in the Papias-matter justice may have to be done. Tischendorf, for example, came within sight of the correct interpretation in the following passage[2]:

Rufinus translates the word λόγια according to the old linguistic usage by *oracula*. It is in the highest degree probable that in fact the book of Papias, according to the Millenarian standing-point of the man, was dedicated especially to prophecies of the Lord. Christian linguistic usage, however, gave the word a wider signification, so that the Sayings of the Lord and of the Apostles, even when they had not the particular character of prophecy, were so called, and Holy Scripture was designated θεία λόγια.

The statement should have stopped with the first sentence. The second sentence is meant to safeguard the supposed reference of Papias to the Gospels!

We have now sufficiently discussed those who have written on the same theme as we have done in the present volume. Our references to them are in the nature of postscripts, made with the object of showing

> That all, as in some piece of art,
> Is toil co-operant to an end.

[1] *Ibid.* 186, 187.

[2] Tischendorf, *Wann wurden,* p. 102; quoted in *Supernatural Religion,* vol. I. 465.

GENERAL INDEX

INDEX LOCORUM

Cambridge:
PRINTED BY J. B. PEACE, M.A.,
AT THE UNIVERSITY PRESS